COMMON CAUSE

COMMONWEALTH SCOTS AND THE GREAT WAR

Stuart Allan and David Forsyth

National Museums Scotland

COMMON CAUSE

Commonwealth Scots
and the Great War

Exhibition at:

National Museum of
Scotland
Chambers Street
Edinburgh EH1 1JF

www.nms.ac.uk

11 July 2014 to
12 October 2014

Supported by:

The Scottish
Government
Riaghaltas na h-Alba

homecomingscotland.com

LED BY **IWM**

Lottery Grants Board
Te Puna Tahua
LOTTO FUNDS FOR YOUR COMMUNITY

Published by
NMS Enterprises Limited – Publishing
a division of NMS Enterprises Limited
National Museums of Scotland
Chambers Street
Edinburgh EH1 1JF

www.nms.ac.uk

Text © National Museums Scotland 2014.

Photographs and illustrations © as credited.

**British Library Cataloguing in
Publication Data**

A catalogue record of this book is available
from the British Library.

ISBN: 978 1 905267 91 0

Publication layout and design by
    NMS Enterprises Limited – Publishing.
Cover design by Mark Blackadder.
Cover images: front – 4th South African
    Infantry dancing at Rouen, June 1918
    (© Ditsong National Museum of Military
    History); back – Pipers and Drummers of
    the New Zealand Expeditionary Force,
    Salisbury Plain, England, May 1917 (©
    Australian War Memorial AWM H16669).
While every effort has been made to locate
    sources of images, if any have been
    inadvertently missed, please contact the
    Publisher.
Printed and bound in the United Kingdom
    by Martins the Printers Ltd, Berwick upon
    Tweed.

For a full listing of
NMS Enterprises Limited – Publishing
titles and related merchandise visit:

www.nms.ac.uk/books

CONTENTS

ACKNOWLEDGEMENTS

This book, and the exhibition it accompanies, owes much to the generosity, work and support of colleagues and friends in cultural, governmental and military organisations in several countries, who are named below and for whom full and proper acknowledgement would require many pages. The authors would first like to express their thanks to the *Common Cause* exhibition project team at National Museums Scotland ably led by Sarah Teale, including Adrienne Breingan on whose picture research and meticulous organisation this book has relied. We are also grateful to Kate Blackadder and Margaret Wilson of NMS Enterprises Limited Publishing and Picture Library divisions, our colleagues in NMS Library, our Director of Collections Jane Carmichael for her foreword and her support for the project, and George Dalgleish and our immediate colleagues in the Department of Scottish History and Archaeology for their tolerance of our distraction, especially to Elaine Edwards for her service overseas.

In Canada: the Honourable Linda Reid MLA Speaker of the Legislative Assembly of British Columbia, Craig James, Gary Lenz, Roger McGuire, Rob MacDonald, Dave Strachan, Lieutenant Colonel Alan Best, Captain Wenzel Taylor, Stephen Otto, Heather McNabb, Bruce Bolton, Earl Chapman, Nicholas Clarke, Shannon Bettles, David Boulding, Paul Ferguson, D. M. Drysdale, Legislative Assembly of British Columbia, Canadian War Museum, Chilliwack Museum, McCord Museum, 48th Highlanders of Canada, Canadian Scottish Regiment (Princess Mary's), Black Watch (Royal Highland Regiment) of Canada, Seaforth Highlanders of Canada.

In Australia: Craig Tibbitts, Dr Brendan Nelson, Captain Ryan Bell, Captain Lionel Baxter, Anthony McAleer, Moya McFadzean, Australian War Memorial, State Library of Victoria, 5/6th Battalion Royal Victoria Regiment.

In New Zealand: Rose Young, Seán Brosnahan, Hazel Crichton, Brent Sutherland, Zoe Richardson, Major Peter Amyes, Auckland War Memorial Museum, Otago Settlers Museum, Otago Southland Company 2nd/4th Royal New Zealand Infantry Regiment.

In South Africa: Lieutenant Colonel E. J. Watson (for his hospitality as well as his professional advice), Sandi Mackenzie, Sergeant Piper Rodney Muller, Gerald Prinsloo, Peter Digby, Major Ian Long, Lieutenant Colonel Bryan Sterne, Captain Francois Morkel, Colonel William Endley, Ditsong National Museum of Military History, Transvaal Scottish Regimental Association and Museum, Cape Town Highlanders, Castle of Good Hope, South African National Defence Force Documentation Centre.

Home shores furth of Scotland: Andrew Parsons (whose support has been crucial), Colonel D. Rankin-Hunt, Lesley Frater, Nicola Frater, Cliff Pettit, John Sheen, London Scottish Regimental Museum, Fusiliers Museum of Northumberland, the Hon. Gordon Campbell Canadian High Commissioner to the United Kingdom, Gabriel Araujo, the Rt Hon. Sir Lockwood Smith New Zealand High Commissioner to the United Kingdom, Rob Taylor, Ceilidh Dunphy, the Hon Alexander Downer Australian High Commissioner to the United Kingdom, the Hon. Mike Rann.

Home shores in Scotland: Lieutenant-Colonel W. J. Blythe, Major A. J. L. Hempenstall, Major J. P. L. Kilpatrick, Carole Wilson, Jane Anderson, Patrick Watt, Jenn Nelson, Allan Carswell, Lieutenant Colonel R. M. Riddell, Emma Halford-Forbes, Jamie Steed, Ruth Steele, Carole Robinson, Norman Drummond, David Matthew, Douglas and Ruth Wilson, Royal Scots Museum, Royal Scots Borderers 1st Battalion Royal Regiment of Scotland, Black Watch Museum, Blair Castle Estates, National Library of Scotland.

Finally, the authors humbly acknowledge the support and encouragement of Fiona and Suzanne respectively, who now know more about this subject than they might have cared to.

FOREWORD

JANE CARMICHAEL

Director of Collections
NATIONAL MUSEUMS SCOTLAND

One hundred years later and with no surviving veterans, the First World War has moved out of reach of living memory. In *Common Cause*, we draw on objects, images and archives to demonstrate the response to and the individual experience of war from an enormous body of individuals, the Scottish diaspora. We aim to portray some of the emotional and historical stories which represent the diversity of participants, their sense of identity, their own view of nationhood and the enormity of the event. To do this, we have drawn on our own and international collections.

These stories help to bridge the gap between ourselves and a time when the world map was drawn very differently. The British empire was dominant and society functioned in a very different way, not least because of the much slower pace of communication across the globe. In an age where the home country might seem physically remote to its emigrants, there was an astonishingly rapid and continuous response to the call to arms. *Common Cause* examines what this meant in terms of perceived loyalties. It is apparent that beyond home and family, a strong sense of Scottish identity and allegiance to their original roots drove many volunteers, Scots abroad and those of Scottish descent, to enlist at the outbreak of war and to support the cause throughout the long years of fighting.

Common Cause also explores the complex relationship between Scottish identity and the emerging national identities of the former British empire. As the excitement and optimism of 1914 gave way to the grim reality of years of conflict, the human cost of fighting the First World War became a foundation of national consciousness – for Canada at Vimy Ridge, for Australia and New Zealand at Gallipoli, for South Africa at Delville Wood – these were emotive and defining national experiences.

We are especially grateful to those organisations in Australia, Canada, New Zealand and South Africa which have lent iconic material: the Australian War Memorial, the Legislative Assembly of

Opposite page:

Canadian troops march down Princes Street, Edinburgh, 1919.

© National Museums Scotland

British Columbia, Auckland War Memorial Museum Tāmaki Paenga Hira, and Ditsong Museums of South Africa National Museum of Military History. Additional support from the Scottish Government and the New Zealand Lottery Grants Board Te Puna Tahua helped to make these loans possible. Museums and military collections in the United Kingdom have also generously lent exhibits.

The exhibition at the National Museum of Scotland is a key element of our major programme of exhibitions and events commemorating the First World War centenary. This accompanying publication provides further historical narrative and analysis on the individual stories and national responses. It brings together the different disciplines of military history and diaspora studies, in an excellent example of the stimulus offered by the wide-ranging collections of National Museums Scotland.

We hope both exhibition and publication will contribute to the understanding of what is being commemorated.

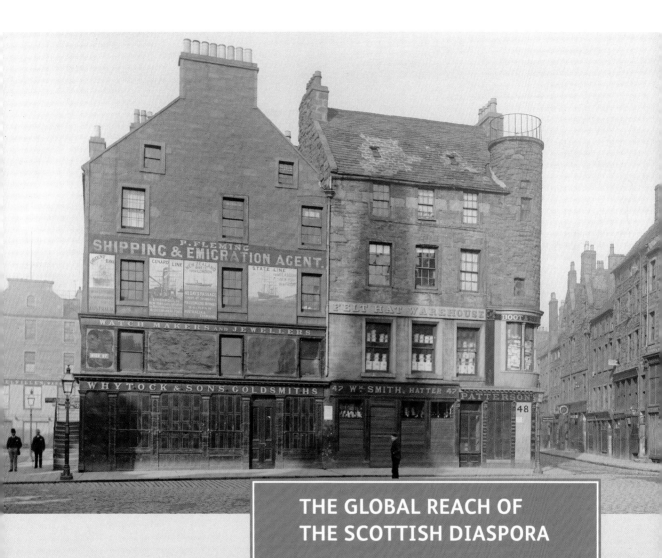

THE GLOBAL REACH OF
THE SCOTTISH DIASPORA

The Scottish diaspora: destinations and impact

Go into whatever country you will, you will always find Scotchmen. They penetrate into every climate: you meet them in all the various departments of travellers, soldiers, merchants, adventurers and domestics ....

Edward Topham, *Letters from Edinburgh*, 1775

ALTHOUGH THIS COMMENT WAS MADE BY AN ENGLISH journalist resident in Edinburgh during the Scottish Enlightenment, it holds true for the continuing experience of Scots in the latter years of the nineteenth century right up until the outbreak of the Great War in August 1914. During this period the Scots were still an exceptionally mobile people. There is a large body of evidence, both anecdotal and empirical, for the Scottish diaspora's ability to permeate all aspects of society in the British Dominions and colonies which today are nations of the Commonwealth. Even Sir Wilfrid Laurier, the great francophone Primer Minister of Canada, stated in 1893 that 'were I not French, I would choose to be a Scot'.[1] Not only did Scots abound, clearly being Scottish brought with it a certain cache to which others aspired.

David Macrae of Gourock, the controversial United Presbyterian Church minister who made a number of lecture tours of North America in the late 1870s on temperance and social reform, noted that, 'I begin to think that either the world was very small or Scotland very large.'[2] No less a figure than Andrew Carnegie, that giant of the Victorian value of self-help and possibly Scotland's most famous emigrant, was convinced that America 'would have been a poor show were it not for the Scotch [*sic*]'.[3] Well, he would say that.

More empirically, other commentators pointed out that the influence of the Scots was universal at the time. Books such as W. J. Rattray's *The Scot in North America* (1880), pointed to a world which was dominated by Scottish culture and values. These were held to range from education, that great Scottish shibboleth and touchstone of social progress; through to Presbyterianism; to the dominance of Scots in the professions, particularly medicine; to Caledonian business acumen; and finally to Scottish intellectual endeavour in the universities. Many of these institutions adopted the Scottish model of a broad approach to tertiary education, with an emphasis on a philosophical element to the curriculum.[4] Of course, there were also dissenting voices that were quick to point out the more negative traits of the Caledonians. An abiding image of the Scot abroad was of someone who was shrewd, clannish and more likely than most to be successful in business or a productive

Opening page:

Gable end of a shipping and emigration agent with destination posters, High Street, Dundee, 1889.

© Dundee City Council Central Library, Photographic Collection, Licensor www.scran.ac.uk

farmer. However, through a form of 'kailyard' internationalism, these traits were promoted from within the Scottish community itself.[5]

The word 'diaspora' is from Greek, meaning 'a scattering'. In current usage 'diaspora' signifies a dispersion of, or the global reach of, an ethnic group or nation through the process of emigration, a process which can be either forced or voluntary. Numbered among the classic diasporic groups are the Jews, Irish, English, Chinese, Palestinians, Armenians – and there is every reason to include the Scots within this category. Professor Tom Devine has identified two significant, if not unique, features which make the Scots stand out amongst the diasporic nations of the world.[6] First, the Scottish diaspora's longevity has been a striking characteristic. Although this book is concerned with migration in the era of the Great War, we have to see this immediate pattern of mobility within a continuum of Scots on the move from the thirteenth century right down to the middle years of the twentieth. This migratory impulse continues to the present day, although the volume and intensity of that flow has ebbed significantly in more recent decades.

The second noteworthy characteristic is the quite remarkable geographical spread of the Scottish diaspora. No continent was insusceptible to contact with the Scots. Outward movement in the early-modern period began in the Low Countries and the Baltic world and, closer to home, in the 'Plantation' of Ulster, mainly from the south-west of Scotland, and then turned south towards England. The great shift occurred when Scottish overseas interests turned away from the North Sea world towards the Atlantic world, where the Caribbean and the Americas offered up a whole continent full of opportunities.

This phenomenon was not confined to the northern hemisphere. Heading south and east to Asia, Africa and the Antipodes, the Scots continued to punch well above their weight in light of their relative size, permeating the British empire in the manner noticed by Topham in North America. Unsurprisingly, Scottish involvement at the core of the imperial endeavour served to aid and abet further their diasporic encroachment. By the later 19th century, the Scots had also penetrated those areas of the world known to economic historians as Britain's 'informal empire', an expansion into areas of Asia and Latin America by British trading and manufacturing interests. In light of the highly commercial nature of this informal empire, it was unsurprising to find Scots at the vanguard in the push for new markets for Britain's industrial and commercial outputs.

The mobility of the Scottish people has often been stereotyped as the forced expulsion of the destitute. Other commentators have noted the Scottish propensity to emigrate as a simple demographic safety valve, which served only to release society from the pressures of poverty, unemployment and political agitation.[7] In reality, emigration has been a much more complex, multi-layered experience and crucially one of the most constant phenomena of Scotland's history, from the medieval period right down to the middle years of the twentieth century.

Between 1825 and 1938, 2,332,608 people left Scotland in search of a new life overseas.[8] However, further analysis of this absolute figure reveals a key proportionate statistic for emigration which must have had a huge impact on Scotland itself. According to pioneering demographic historian Michael Flinn, this total represents Scotland losing over half of its natural increase in population through emigration during the course of this period.[9] This figure places Scotland as one of the three topmost 'exporters' of people from Europe, with Ireland taking first place in what Flinn described as an 'unenviable championship'.

By 1914 emigration from Scotland had reached one of its periodic peaks. The Scottish economy was dominated by industries highly dependent on export markets; this was dangerous; Scotland became very susceptible to the vagaries of the international economy.[10] This concentration is observed very starkly in statistics such as the fact that by 1914 a third of the British shipping tonnage, which represented almost a fifth of the world's output, had been built on Glasgow's River Clyde.[11] Emigration was the human dimension of these trading connections of the era's maritime-based international economy.

The last decades of the nineteenth century and into the first decade of the twentieth were a dynamic time for Scotland. The Dominions of

Right:

Cunard liner RMS *Aquitania* under construction at John Brown & Company, Clydebank, *c.*1913.

© National Maritime Museum, Greenwich, London

Canada, Australia, New Zealand and South Africa were the recipients of over 40% of British capital.[12] This helped to cement both British identity and influence within these countries, even at a time when many non-British emigrants sought the benefits of emigration to the countries of the British Commonwealth. The global reach of Scottish capital was an integral part of this international investment. The opening decades of the twentieth century saw a continuation of the 'High Noon of Empire', the apogee of British imperialism fuelled by a massive outpouring of capital, partly underwritten by the small-scale investments of the middle class.

One distinctive feature of the great haemorrhage of Scots during the years immediately prior to the outbreak of the First World War was the challenge raised by Dominions to the United States' position as the main destination of choice for Scottish emigrants. The United States had welcomed the largest numbers of Scotland's 'huddled masses' with the advent of transatlantic steamship travel in the late 1850s.[13] In the four years before the war, 51.95% of Scottish overseas emigrants left for Canada, while the total departing for Australasia almost doubled during the same short period.[14] Clearly the former 'tyranny of distance' of the three-month voyage under sail was no longer a bar to Scotland's emigrant population. This passage was of course smoothed by the speedier more comfortable travel afforded by steamships. The intensity of this outward flow was reminiscent of the 'epidemical fury of emigration' which Samuel Johnson and James Boswell encountered during their travels around Skye and Raasay in 1773.[15]

Between 1900 and 1904 South Africa had secured just a little over 20% of those Scots in search of a new homeland. However, in the ten years up to the outbreak of the Great War these numbers reverted to their more usual percentage position in single figures. South Africa seems to have been a favoured destination for middle-class Scots.[16]

The Canadian government in particular made concerted efforts to attract migrants in the early years of the twentieth century. This was no doubt spurred on by the continuing move to the west which had begun in the early 1890s, in the main by internal migration from Ontario in eastern Canada. This population shift was encouraged by the official accession of the prairie provinces of Alberta and Saskatchewan to the Dominion in 1905. There was a racial dimension to all this. Government emigration schemes were often targeted, with favouritism shown to settlers from Britain over the 'motley crowd' leaving southern Europe with their equal hopes of opportunity and new beginnings. By 1911, Canada was home to around 7.2 million people, with the majority, 6.4 million, born in Britain. The Scottish phalanx was a significant and influential proportion of this population.

The nature of the Scottish emigrant population is telling and here a Scottish particularism comes to light. It is not until 1912 that the method of reporting emigrant departures allowed modern historical demographers to decipher more accurately the occupational and social structure of Scotland's emigrant population. The startling indictment on the ability of Scottish society to retain its workforce is that some 47% of adult males leaving Scotland in 1912 and 1913 were described as skilled.[17] To put this into perspective, this was 11% more than the equivalent occupational group which left England and Wales at the same time. These figures provide an insight into the nature of Scottish diasporic communities during this period. This social group was educated, skilled and in search of cultural association.

Drilling down into these figures, the structure of Scottish emigrant communities significantly differed between each of the new destinations. Perhaps surprisingly, the unskilled labouring group was relatively high in Canada where 39% of Scottish emigrant workers belonged to this group. This contrasts with the overall proportion of unskilled labourers which stood at 29% of the total number of Scotsmen leaving in 1912 and 1913. However, at 41% of work-age Scotsmen, Australasia attracted the largest proportion of the unskilled.[18]

What is abundantly clear from these statistics is that the overwhelming majority of Scottish emigrants during this period were urban Lowlanders, urban with an intimate experience of the processes of industrialisation which had occurred in Scottish society. Thanks to the critical mass that had developed around Glasgow and its surrounding hinterland, Scotland was propelled to become known as the 'workshop of the word'. This is the root of the 'great paradox' of Scottish emigration.[19] Unlike the rest of Europe, which experienced a drain from the rural sector of society, the unprecedented exposure of Scotland to the twin forces of industrialisation and urbanisation brought with it a very particular array of social, health and housing problems. This triumvirate might have been the cause which acted to expel so many people from what looked to be, in pure economic terms, a mature and successful industrial economy. Behind this phenomenon lies the very intense nature of that experience of modernisation. As the rest of the world made strides to catch up with Britain, there was a continual demand not merely for the finished goods of the first industrial nation, but also an almost insatiable need for its human output in the form of emigrants.

During the great exodus from Scotland between 1841 and 1911, around 600,000 Scots left for their larger southern neighbour, to create a 'near diaspora'.[20] Although this figure includes Wales, the vast majority settled in England. Often overlooked or ignored in studies of

Scottish migration, the Scottish diaspora in England was significant, particularly within a number of the major English urban and industrial enclaves. These areas were indeed to become fertile recruiting grounds for the Scottish units raised in and around English cities at the start of the Great War. However, as one might expect, it was the pull of the imperial capital, London, which attracted many of Scotland's south-ward-bound migrants. The 1911 census revealed a Scots-born population in England of 321,825. Around 100,000 of this total were to be found in the Greater London area, seduced by the lure of metropolitan migrant success, or the prize of a house in the capital's Home County environs.[21]

For the aspiring Scottish middle-class migrants, the south-east may have been perceived as the prime destination, especially as Scots maintained a high profile within the higher echelons of metropolitan society. But for most it was the classic pull of higher wages and the demand for their industrial specialisms that took them south in such significant numbers. Therefore the structurally similar industrial enclaves of both Northumberland and County Durham were a consistent attraction for the persistently migratory Scottish artisan skilled élites and their semi-skilled comrades.

Thus on the eve of the Great War, the overwhelming concentration of Scots was in the industrial north, where a mere few per cent short of three-quarters of the total Scottish population in England and Wales were to be found. Within that concentration of settlement was yet another critical mass. Of these, most had left the counties surrounding three of Scotland's major urban enclaves of Glasgow, Edinburgh and Aberdeen.

Well before the Great War, Scotland had emerged as one of Europe's, and therefore the world's, most highly urbanised societies; an overwhelming four-fifths of the Scottish population was crowded into the narrow strip of land which formed the industrial heartland of the central lowlands. By 1911 nearly 60% of Scots lived in settlements with a population of 5000 or over.[22] This period of urbanisation mirrored the sea-change in industrialisation when textiles were replaced as the dynamic sector of the Scottish economy by the classic heavy industrial triumvirate of engineering, steelmaking and shipbuilding.

During the early years of the twentieth century, the first contact which future emigrants would have had with their new homeland came through the countrywide tours, conducted with an almost evangelistic fervour, by itinerant emigration agents. This was the 'pull' factor at its most powerful. Agents and representatives of different Commonwealth countries competed with each other to advocate and promote the relative attractions and benefits of the country of their paymasters.

After the enthusiasm of the agent himself, the technology of the time in the form of the simple lantern slide became the means of enticing prospective recruits into making a decision to leave. Each prospective destination country was well-armed for this battle for the hearts and minds of prospective emigrants: by 1912 New Zealand's Department of Immigration had 3000 such slides in its armoury.[23] Agents were told to concentrate on rural counties and to prioritise the recruitment of farm servants, particularly those who could prove themselves as financially independent. However, the most effective promoters of emigration were often the emigrants themselves; kin and patronage networks continued to play a pivotal role in the whole process.

The new Dominion of Canada, galvanised by its Confederation of 1871, took the lead in encouraging settlement, and the federal government backed this up with a large budget to fund the promotional campaign to entice Scots to Canada, especially to help populate the expansive prairie provinces.[24] Government offices were set up in Scotland's main cities with oversight of the peripatetic agents who recruited on behalf of both the federal Dominion government and the provincial governments. If that competition between central government and the provinces was not enough, they had to pitch their case against the best efforts of American and Antipodean recruitment. Canada stationed resident government emigration agents in Glasgow in 1880, followed by Aberdeen in 1907.

In the latter years of the nineteenth century there arose an impression in some quarters of a growing gender imbalance in the composition of those leaving Scotland. To counteract this notion, a number of specialist agencies sprang up, specifically aimed at the promotion of female emigration, enticing young women to emigrate as domestic servants. This would be an experience of employment which was very similar to the situation at home. However, emigration brought with it a sense of optimism, and organisations such as the Aberdeen Ladies Union were established to recruit, train and then ship abroad young Scottish ladies. These were women who were in search of employment, improvement and perhaps a husband, and a strong element of social engineering was prevalent among those who ran such organised emigration schemes. Perhaps this really was required: the demographic reality was that, between 1861 and 1911, male emigrants did indeed outnumber the number of females leaving Scotland.

In this survey of emigrant pathways which led to destinations within the British empire, we must not overlook the obdurate reality that from 1865 to 1910, despite some blips, the persistent favoured destination for most Scottish emigrants was the United States of America. Again, the most notable feature of this outward flow to the

United States was the over-representation of those who had left from the industrial heartland.[25] Though many members of Scotland's overwhelmingly urban emigrant population had reaped some of the rewards of improved standards of living, they were also making a conscious, well thought through, decision to leave. This human haemorrhage from industrial Scotland did not represent, as with other European societies, a flight from destitution and dislocation.[26]

Scottish emigration to Australia meanwhile displayed an overwhelming religious cohesion in favour of Presbyterianism, with some 85% of mid-nineteenth century Protestant Scots settlers describing themselves as such.[27] The Scots in Australia make for a fascinating study of an ethnic group who on the surface would appear to have made an impact on that nation far in excess of their relative numbers. From the early squatters (those who grazed their livestock on Crown land without due legal claim), to becoming major landholders, and finally as the successful entrepreneurs who so successfully propelled the Australian agricultural economy, Scots seemed to be at the fore. Equally, Australia's cities and rapidly developing industrial enclave, were thralled to Scottish entrepreneurial influence, specifically in the more innovative sectors of the engineering and manufacturing industries.

Traditionally the tone of emigrant histories was celebratory and lauded the success stories. The shadow of Andrew Carnegie, that most pre-eminent of Scottish emigrants, was cast far across the Scottish diasporic world, reaching as far as Australia. Some commentators have noted a tendency to celebrate the role of the 'great man' in Australian diasporic biography.[28] This might have helped to obscure the fact that the origins of most Scottish emigrants to Australia were working class. The drives to recruit new settlers by Australian agents were much more centralised than the more multi-dimensional campaigns by Canada carried out from the end of the nineteenth century into the early years of the twentieth.

Although both countries were organised on the principle of federalism, it was only Canada which allowed direct recruitment by its Provinces. The Government of the Dominion of Australia was the lead agency for the promotion of Australia as an emigrant destination. Additionally, emigration agency activity was devolved within Great Britain. Canada had resident federal agents based at key cities throughout the British Isles, while the Australians preferred to run their emigration campaign from London with no input from the individual state governments which had come together to form the Commonwealth of Australia. When the colonies federated in 1901, control of immigration changed. Instead of each former colony managing its own system, the Commonwealth now oversaw recruiting and selection. This is all the more surprising given the fairly aggressive recruitment policies pursued by the former independent colonies, especially Queensland which in the 1880s had caused no little concern to the Canadian agents.[29]

Scottish emigration to South Africa was very different from the other British Dominions in one major respect: quite simply, it never experienced the same levels of mass emigration as the other countries.[30] With a few notable exceptions, in 1895–99 and 1900–1904 South Africa was consistently the least popular choice for Scottish emigrants.[31] Though relatively small in proportion to the other European migrant groups in South Africa, the Scots who went there were still very conscious of their Scottish identity, expressing this through a vigorous associational life, such as the Cape Town Caledonian Society established in 1881.[32] The number of Scots leaving for South Africa only comfortably reached four figures in the period 1895–99. Between 1900 and 1904, South Africa received around 20% of the total of Scottish emigrants, a surge which saw the annual average rise to over 5550 emigrants choosing it as their new home. The increase would appear to have been at the expense of emigration to Australia, the proportion of emigrants to which plummeted to single figures between 1890 and 1909.[33]

Of all Dominion destinations for Scottish emigrants, it was South Africa which displayed the most markedly unequal gender ratio, with a ratio of nearly three men to every woman. This is probably best explained by the commercial development of the gold and diamond mines. The world of the mining settlements was an overwhelmingly masculine one. It was the domination of the mining industry and the prospect of enrichment in the gold-fields which attracted so many unaccompanied males. This also explains the rather transitory nature of Scottish migration to South Africa during this period, and the creation of a Scottish diaspora community made up of 'sojourners' or temporary migrants.

Indeed the number of migrants returning to Scotland from the colony almost equalled the number of those arriving, a tendency mirrored in the experience of English emigrants. Some commentators have suggested that all was not well in South Africa, however.[34] There is some evidence that South Africa acted as the first step in the demographic phenomenon known as step migration[35] – that is, when migration is sequential. The next step often would be the voyage further south to the Antipodes and hopefully to a more permanent home.

Why did Scottish society display such a propensity to outward migration? Even in those years when overseas emigration was at a lower overall level, Scottish migration to England and Wales tended to increase. Was this phenomenon a reflection of markedly aspirational people who by accident of birth were born in a society with limited resources and opportunity? Or were the Scots characteristically more mobile, determined to take advantage of any opportunity, regardless of the distance of that potential new location? A range of subjective factors was in play, but migration was also self-perpetuating since, if they desired , Scottish emigrants could reasonably expect to receive a warm welcome from fellow Scots already settled overseas.

The associational culture of the Scottish diaspora

During his celebrated tour of the Scottish highlands and the Hebrides in 1773, Samuel Johnson received this answer from a tenant farmer from Glenmoriston, Inverness-shire, when asked whether or not he would like to emigrate: 'No man willingly left his native country'.[36] In one sense, Scots emigrants did not need to leave their native country, since its culture and traditions could be taken with them and played out in the diasporic context. The intricate, often labyrinthine, and at times internecine nature of the numerous Scottish clubs and societies which emerged within the emigrant scene has become one of the most visible and powerful manifestations of Scottish diasporic identity. The sphere of associational culture provided new emigrants with substitutes for the family and kinship links they had often left at home. Association-alism took on a variety of manifestations among the most prominent examples were the St Andrew's societies, Caledonian clubs, Scottish societies; and of course, for the devotees of the Scotland's national bard, the ubiquitous Burns clubs.

Above:

48th Highlanders of Canada celebrate Queen Victoria's Diamond Jubilee at Winchester, Ontario, 1897.

© National Museums Scotland

11

The activities of the members of such associations could be described as 'performing their connection to Scotland'. Association-alism allowed Scots to remain close to the culture and institutions of their homeland, despite the great geographical separation, and to declare themselves Scottish.

Emigration societies, government bodies and recruitment agents offered only the most basic level of assistance and aftercare for migrants on arrival in the new country. From the manly prowess of sporting clubs and highland games to the literary activities of Burns Clubs, associationalism could be purely social. However, practical help was also at hand for the needy through the plethora of St Andrew's and Caledonian societies that took up the cudgels for their deserving, newly arrived fellow countrymen and their families whose first experience of the emigration was that of difficulty or distress.

Associationalism is a useful method of 'measuring' Scottishness. It is the easily the most quantifiable, in simple terms of number of organ-isations or the levels of individual participation. Of course, by empha-sising the role of associational culture there is a danger of excluding the great numbers of Canadians, Australians, New Zealanders or South Africans with Scottish ancestry who were not actively involved in Scottish associational life. Was the Scottish diaspora's associational behaviour especially exaggerated? Did it really represent a major change from the situation back home in Scotland?

There were plenty of Scots who fully embraced new identities and accepted new cultural mores; neither St Andrew nor Burns would form part of their identity, culture or leisure time. Those Scots who did not participate in associationalism might be termed the 'invisible emigrants', an expression first coined by Charlotte Erickson, historian of nineteenth-century English and Scottish emigration to the United States.[37] This term originally described the way in which many emi-grants speedily and unobtrusively entered the mainstream of life in their new homeland.

As diasporic communities aged, and the immediacy of any direct genetic link to Scotland became increasingly remote, the pure ethnic qualification for membership of Scottish associations had to be diluted over time to ensure the very survival of associationalism itself. The decline of the qualification of ethnic purity can be charted in one of the north-east of England's most notable Burns Clubs.[38] By the turn of the twentieth century this organisation had to submit to the inevitable and made the decision to admit to membership mere 'admirers' of Scotland's national bard, regardless of either birth-place or blood-line.

The challenge to the diasporic Scots, a challenge which also had to be confronted by Scottish communities overseas, was to find a means of

Above:

St Andrew's Society Ball,
Windsor Hotel, Montreal,
QC, 1878.

McCord Museum, Montreal
II-51688

preserving those components of ethnic identity which made them distinctively Scottish. This test was less important in the early years of settlement, when associationalism was just that, a simple transplantation of the social and civic worlds in which Scots had participated at home before heading away from Scotland in search of new opportunities.

Associationalism was an important outlet for expressing Scottishness, and should not be dismissed as merely a leisure pursuit for homesick or romantically inclined Scottish émigrés. Membership of Scottish clubs and societies was usually available to all those who could demonstrate their Scottish descent. In recognition of the loosening of direct ties with the homeland, the constitution of at least one St Andrew's society, that of Toronto, specifically allowed membership for the 'children, grandchildren, great-grandchildren, of Natives of Scotland'.[39] Large, influential Scottish associations, such as the St Andrew's Society of Toronto, were generally dominated by local élites: business leaders, lawyers and medical professionals. But having been founded in 1836 as a mainly philanthropic organisation with the principal objective 'the relief of destitute Scotch Emigrants', membership of the Society had to be open to all regardless of their political or religious creeds.

Within the Scottish world there was also a propensity for interest groups to diversify and specialise, reflecting the cultural and geographical nuances of Scotland itself. As far as emigration to New Zealand was concerned, the Scottish cohort consistently represented around 25% of all British-born emigrants to that country from 1861 up until the middle years of the twentieth century. With such a presence there was greater scope to reflect the diversity of Scotland. In New Zealand, a Scottish associational society could afford to be less cohesive.

13

Thus in Dunedin in 1881, a need was felt by prominent members of the Scottish community to form a Gaelic Society of Dunedin. For the founders of this group the existing and well-established network of Scottish associationalism was perceived as insufficient for the cultural and social requirements of the growing body of emigrants from the Scottish highlands to Dunedin and its Otago hinterland.[40]

The rise of Scottish clubs and societies in their various guises had wider ramifications for the way in which Scots negotiated their way through the business and professional connections of a new society. The technical term often used to encapsulate the complexities of associationalism is 'social capital', describing the individual and collective value and self-interest inherent in the pattern and intensity of networks among people, and the shared values which arise from those who operate within such networks. Social capital need not be a pejorative term: the concept has many positive aspects, most visibly demonstrated in the philanthropic founding principles of many of the early St Andrew's societies. A more insidious trait might be the selective use of social capital to influence self-advancement, or to seek or dispense patronage. At worst this might be to the detriment of those who fall outwith the narrow confines of the community or group.

Military associationalism lay between these two worlds. As this book will go on to demonstrate, the numerous regiments and units of Scottish origin were more than just a colourful adjunct of military service or local militia organisation.[41] Scottish military associationalism represented a sphere where differences in class and income could be accommodated within the unity of common purpose. Local military service, with its formal command structure, allowed Scots to act as a 'band of brothers' in terms of ethnic unity, while observing the strictures of social class represented in the rank system. It emerged in the context of the military volunteering movement, revived in Great Britain itself in the late 1850s. Part-time military units of a similar nature appeared soon afterwards in British imperial possessions across the world.[42]

As Scottish associationalism developed, it naturally adapted to the prevailing culture or social nuances of the host nation. In the sporty outdoors culture of New Zealand, Caledonian (or highland) Games fostered by the network of Caledonian societies became a key public manifestation of Scottishness. But these very public expressions of Scottishness were not necessarily the sign of a confident community. Often the reality was quite the opposite; it was the performance of a community in search of ethnic cohesion in the face of new waves of emigration from other nationalities which the Scots perceived as being in direct competition to themselves. As time passed, greater assimilation was inevitable and the need to seek sustentation for the home

Left:

Men of the Victorian
Scottish Regiment,
Australia, 1908.

© National Museums
Scotland

culture increased. The challenge for Scottish communities was to preserve their distinctive mores, customs and traditions, while simultaneously they had to make a full contribution to the emergent culture of their new homeland.

Some commentators have warned about the tendency of associations to perpetuate and generate exclusivity and division: associational culture has at times been accused of promoting discord and intolerance. Scottish associationalism, however, with its colourful displays of pipe bands or highland games, could overcome this by dint of its wider popularity as public spectacle and, significantly, its high recognition factor in the culture of war. In the case of Australia and New Zealand in 1914, where overseas military units were organised solely in the image of the Commonwealth country itself, and without any formal reference to ethnic distinctiveness, it did not take long for Scottishness to reappear in its most popular form.

This was exemplified in New Zealand when, on 12 October 1914, the *Otago Daily Times* reported that the Caledonian Society of Otago had supplied the Otago Infantry Battalion with the instruments necessary to form a fully-equipped pipe band as a means of 'recognising the sentimental and romantic value of bagpipe music'. Although this was an area with strong Scottish connections, the battalion in question was not exclusively Scottish in formal identity or recruitment profile; and yet a newspaper could report that 'every officer and man was grateful for the gift' without complaint or controversy.[43]

Scottish distinctiveness was initially nurtured and sustained, however, both within the emigrant home, and in the public sphere in the

Above:

Pipes and drums of the
Otago Infantry Battalion,
September 1914.

**Photograph courtesy of
Otago Witness**

context of religious affiliation. Thus, as was the situation in Scotland, religious life offered an outlet not merely for expressing personal faith, but also more widely for associational and recreational activities. Religion, particularly though not exclusively Presbyterianism in its various hues, was an important component of Scottish diasporic identity. Having taken up his ministry in 1902 at St Columba's, Pont Street (one of two Church of Scotland congregations in London) the newly appointed minister wrote that 'we are all exiled Scots' who were loyal to their Church of 'whose worship we love and whose traditions we are proud to inherit'.[44]

Although the statistics presented at the start of this introduction reveal the huge quantitative effect of mass emigration on Scottish society, it must be borne in mind that throughout the course of the nineteenth century Scots only made up 8% of emigrants from the British Isles. This percentage does of course include the huge exodus from Scotland's Celtic near-neighbour Ireland, which had a very different experience of emigration. However, in direct contrast to its larger southern neighbour, the propensity of Scots to emigrate was consistently twice that of their English contemporaries. In their propensity to associational culture, and in the visibility of the outward display of identity, the Scots of course also excelled.

The modest ambition of most emigrants was rewarded by modest success; the historiography of Scottish emigration has seen a major sea-change in recent years. It has moved on from polemical denouncement of the clearance of the destitute and the blind celebration of achievements of the successful or even the infamous.[45] Contemporary emigration studies now offer a more sophisticated analysis of the many influences which have initiated and shaped that constant nationwide exodus from Scotland. Within the diaspora countries there are now university research programmes and centres dedicated to the exploration of the nature of the Scottish diaspora in the host country.[46] The story of Commonwealth Scots and the Great War properly sits within this broad and complex historical phenomenon. The story is already a matter of record, but is usually embodied only in the names of individuals and units which appear in regimental and operational histories of the military annals of the countries concerned.

Unprecedented levels of emigration during the early years of the twentieth century had served to boost the Scottish population of the countries of today's Commonwealth. Many young men who were a part of this outward movement unexpectedly found themselves in 1914 returning to fight for a homeland which they thought they had left behind. The present study, viewed from Scotland, and written in the centenary year of the outbreak of the First World War, seeks to draw together strands of experience from across the Scottish diaspora in order to explore the expressions of multiple identity which emerged in the extraordinary context of a world war.

Diaspora, associationalism and material culture

Whaur are the bairns she sheltered, the sons she was laith to lose?
When they wandered awa' on the ootwith roads, whaur ever their
fancy chose.

Charles Murray, from 'Wha Bears a Blade for Scotland',
A Sough O' War (London 1917)

The challenge of representing a nation's diaspora in a museum collection within the country of departure is the fact that the 'material culture', which represents that diaspora – the objects – have similarly migrated to, or were created in, the new homeland. It is no coincidence that the five key objects in the *Common Cause* exhibition, which this volume accompanies, were temporarily brought to Scotland for the duration of the exhibition, in an act of friendly cultural 'repatriation'. A set of bagpipes, a regimental mascot, a Victoria Cross gallantry decoration, a piece of commemorative sculpture, and a Communion set used on the battlefield, appear here as the symbolic indicators of this global phenomenon.

Despite the longevity and global reach of the Scottish diaspora, and the demographic impact of migration on Scotland itself, there is still a great paucity of material illustrating emigration within Scottish public collections. The *Scotland* galleries of the National Museum of Scotland include displays which are the sole national focus, beyond academia, of the great outpouring of people from Scotland.[47]

One of the reasons for identifying the importance of association-alism is that this phenomenon creates and disseminates a rich material cultural which is heavily loaded with both identity and cultural symbolism. A study of the material culture of the Irish diaspora in the United States has shown that this ethnic group 'immigrated with entrenched social dispositions and ideologies reflected in objects and material signs'.[48] Thus objects remain a key facet of evidence for both the preservation and shaping of identity in diasporic society, where association-alism reflected 'continued attachment to how life was lived at home'.[49]

What of this diasporic material culture? The plethora of societies and clubs mixed a heady cocktail of St Andrew's eve balls, highland gatherings and, of course, pipe band performances. As both participants and spectators in associational activity there was a requirement for the correct attire, so the demand for tartan and its accoutrements through the 'tribal enthusiasm, by Scots and supposed Scots from Texas to Tokyo' increased the output of the manufacturers of identity.[50]

A brief search of the collections database of one local museum in Ontario, Canada, at the centre of an area in part founded by the efforts of a Scottish land agent and still today a centre of Scottish settlement, revealed 91 records with the search term 'Scottish'.[51] This does not include other searches under keywords such as 'kilt' or 'tartan'. Still the range of material cast up by this search is reflective both of the domestic and associational life of a Scottish diasporic community: from ladles to brooches, via woods (wooden balls) for lawn bowls (then the more visibly Scottish paraphernalia of the local Caledonian society), to a 'kailyard' or kitsch postcard featuring a Highland cow. Add to this collection a book on the religious history of Scotland, and a Psalter to accompany the praise of a Scots Canadian kirk. The haul is rounded off by a set of transparencies of a Scottish country dancer.

It may readily be imagined that this fascinating little collection is far from unique as a snapshot of the material culture of the Scottish diaspora. However, more closely allied to the subject of this book, the selection of the terms 'kilt' or 'tartan' reveals the material evidence for military associationalism in the form of a range of traditional Scottish dress related to local militia units. Unquestionably, 'the rich associational culture' and 'the export of 'integral parts of Scottish civil society' were phenomena which were equally matched by the 'deeply influential Scottish military tradition'.[52]

Notes

1 Stated in a speech by Laurier at Strathroy, Ontario, on 19 September 1908; quoted in McArthur 1919, n.p.
2 Macrae 1908, p. 121.
3 Quoted in *ibid*., p. 123.
4 Tom Brooking, 'Sharing Out the Haggis: The special Scottish contribution to New Zealand history', in Brooking and Coleman (eds.) 2003, p. 60.
5 Macrae 1876, p. 35.
6 Devine 2011, pp. 289–90.
7 One of the earlier, more polemical examples is Mackenzie 1914.
8 Flinn 1977, pp. 441–2.
9 *Ibid*.
10 Devine 2006, pp. 484–5.
11 *Ibid*., p. 61.
12 *Ibid*., pp. 254–5 and 474.
13 Richards 2004, p. 212.
14 Baines 1986, p. 64.
15 Johnson 1775, p. 79.
16 MacKenzie with Dalziel 2007, pp. 216–28.
17 Flinn 1997, p. 452.
18 *Ibid*., p. 453.
19 The term was first used by Campbell 1985, p. 9 and then further developed by T. M. Devine, 'Introduction: The Paradox of Scottish Emigration', in Devine (ed.) 1992, pp. 1–15.
20 Bueltmann, et al. 2013, pp. 154–6; and Flinn 1977, p. 442.
21 Harper 2012, p. 19.
22 *Ibid*., pp. 51–2.
23 *Ibid*., p. 141.
24 Harper 2003, p. 149.
25 Richards 2004, p. 213.
26 Baines 1995, pp. 16–17.
27 Prentis 2008, p. 64.
28 Ian Donnachie, 'The Making of "Scots on the Make": Scottish Settlement and enterprise in Australia, 1830–1900', in Devine 1992, p. 135.
29 This competition between the dominion countries and emigrant recruitment as a 'business' is explored in Harper 2003, ch. 4.
30 MacKenzie with Dalziel 2007, p. 18.
31 Flinn 1977, p. 450.
32 See in particular MacKenzie with Dalziel 2007, ch. 8
33 Bueltmann, *et al*. 2013, p. 68.
34 Flinn 1977, p. 450.
35 Bueltmann *et al*. 2013, pp. 6 and 60.
36 Johnson 1775, p. 79.
37 Erickson 1972.
38 In this instance, the Darlington Burns Association. John A. Burnett, 'Department of Help for Skint Scotsmen!: Associationalism among Scots migrants in the North East of England', in Bueltmann, et al. (eds) 2009, p. 223.
39 Quoted in Shannon O'Connor, '"Nowhere in Canada is St Andrew's Day celebrated with Greater Loyalty and Enthusiasm", Scottish Associational Culture in Toronto, *c*.1836–1914', in Bueltmann, et al. (eds) 2009, p. 102.
40 This excellent example of associational diversification is discussed in Bueltmann 2011, pp. 75–7.
41 Fraser 1900, pp. 10–27 provides an interesting genealogy of the Canadian examples of these units. See also George F. G. Stanley, 'The Scottish Military Tradition', in Reid 1976, pp. 149–50.
42 Wendy Ugolini, 'Scottish Commonwealth Regiments', in Spiers, et al. (eds), pp. 487–90.
43 *Otago Daily Times*, 12 October 1914.
44 Quoted in Harper 2012, p. 41, from Cameron 1979, pp. 179–80.
45 For example, more classically Burton 1864 or more recently Bruce 1996.
46 These are *inter alia* the Centre for Scottish Studies, University of Guelph, Centre for Scottish Studies, Simon Fraser University and the Centre for Irish and Scottish Studies, the University of Otago.
47 John M. MacKenzie, 'A Scottish Empire? The Scottish Diaspora and Interactive Identities', in Brooking and Coleman (eds) 2003, p. 17.
48 Brighton 2009, p. xx.
49 Morton 2012, p. 270.
50 Hugh Trevor-Roper, 'The Invention of Tradition: The Highland Tradition of Scotland', in Hobsbawm and Ranger (eds) 1983, p. 41.
51 Guelph Civic Museum http://guelph.ca/museum/
52 Devine 2011, p. 167.

Bibliography

Baines, Dudley 1986. *Migration in a Mature Economy: Emigration and Internal Migration in England and Wales* (Cambridge).
Baines, Dudley 1995. *Emigration from Europe, 1815–1930* (Cambridge).
Brighton, Stephen A. 2009. *Historical Archaeology of the Irish Diaspora; A Transnational Approach*, Knoxville.

Brooking, Tom and Jennie Coleman (eds) 2003. *The Heather and the Fern: Scottish Migration and New Zealand Settlement* (Dunedin).

Bruce, Duncan A. *c.*1996. *The Mark of the Scots: their astonishing contributions to history, science, democracy, literature and the arts* (Secaucus, NJ).

Bueltmann, Tanja 2011. *Scottish Ethnicity and the Making of New Zealand Society, 1850–1930* (Edinburgh).

Bueltmann, Tanja, Andrew Hinson and Graeme Morton (eds) 2009. *Ties of Bluid, Kin and Countrie: Scottish Associationalism in the Diaspora* (Guelph).

Bueltmann, Tanja, Andrew Hinson and Graeme Morton, 2013. *The Scottish Diaspora* (Edinburgh).

Burton, J. H. 1864. *The Scot Abroad*, 2 vols (Edinburgh).

Cage, R. A. 1985. *The Scots Abroad: Labour, Capital, Enterprise, 1750–1914* (London).

Cameron, George G. 1979. *The Scots Kirk in London* (Oxford).

Devine, T. M. (ed.) 1992. *Scottish Emigration and Society* (Edinburgh).

Devine, T. M. 2006. *The Scottish Nation: 1700–2007* (London), pp. 484–5.

Devine, T. M. 2011. *To the Ends of the Earth: Scotland's Global Diaspora* (London).

Erickson, Charlotte 1972. *Invisible Immigrants; Adaption of English and Scottish Immigrants in Nineteenth century America* (London).

Flinn, Michael (ed.) 1977. *Scottish Population History from the 17th Century to the 1930s* (Cambridge).

Fraser, Alexander 1900. *The 48th Highlanders of Toronto* (Toronto).

Harper, Marjory 2003. *Adventurers and Exiles: The Great Scottish Exodus* (London).

Harper, Marjory 2012. *Scotland No More?: The Scots Who Left Scotland in the Twentieth Century* (Edinburgh).

Hobsbawm, Eric and Terence Ranger (eds) 1983. *The Invention of Tradition* (Cambridge).

Johnson, Samuel 1775. *A Journey to the Western Islands of Scotland*.

McArthur, Peter 1919. *Sir Wilfrid Laurier* (Toronto).

Mackenzie, Alexander 1914. *The History of the Highland Clearances*, 2nd ed. (Stirling).

MacKenzie, John M. with Nigel R. Dalziel 2007. *The Scots in South Africa; Ethnicity, Identity, Gender and Race, 1772–1914* (Manchester).

Macrae, David 1876. *The Americans at Home and Other Papers* (Glasgow).

Macrae, David 1908. *American Presidents and Men I Have Met* (Glasgow).

Morton, Graeme 2012. *Ourselves and Others: Scotland, 1832–1915* (Edinburgh).

Prentis, Malcolm 2008. *The Scots in Australia*, p. 64.

Reid, W. Stanford 1976. *The Scottish Tradition in Canada* (Toronto).

Richards, Eric 2004. *Britannia's Children: Emigration from England, Scotland, Wales and Ireland since 1600* (London and New York).

Spiers, Edward M., Jeremy Crang and Matthew Strickland (eds) 2012. *A Military History of Scotland* (Edinburgh).

MOBILISATION, MEMORY
AND MATERIAL CULTURE

In Flanders fields the poppies blow
Between the crosses, row on row
That mark our place; and in the sky
The larks still bravely singing, fly
Scarce heard amid the guns below.

We are the Dead. Short days ago
We lived, felt dawn, saw sunset glow,
Loved and were loved, and now we lie,
In Flanders fields.

Take up our quarrel with the foe:
To you from failing hands we throw
The torch; be yours to hold it high.
If ye break faith with us who die
We shall not sleep, though poppies grow
In Flanders fields.

CONTEXT IS HARDLY REQUIRED TO RECOGNISE AND acknowledge the outstanding quality of Lieutenant-Colonel John McCrae's poem 'In Flanders Fields' – a reading is sufficient. But the story of its author and its creation offers a useful setting-off point for a book about Scottish emigration and the First World War. Composed during 1914 and 1915 by a medical officer serving on the Western Front, it was published, anonymously, in *Punch* magazine on 8th December 1915 and achieved almost instant popularity. The poet's appeal to keep faith with the dead and finish the job of war resonated with soldiers and civilians alike, earning McCrae the accolades of peers and critics when, with its author named, the poem was widely republished. McCrae's death from pneumonia and meningitis in January 1918 only heightened the poignancy of a poem reputedly written in response to the death of a close friend, at whose makeshift burial McCrae had presided, and its sentiments were surely conceived out of the poet's experiences as a participant in and witness to the Second Battle of Ypres in spring 1915.

The poem's value was recognised in official quarters and it was soon put to work to encourage popular support for the war effort, publicising the sale of war bonds. After the war it appeared widely in print again in literature raising funds for veterans. It inspired the adoption of the artificial poppy worn as a symbol of remembrance, an idea which spread from the American YMCA to the American Legion and on to the British Legion, and which by the late 1920s was firmly

22

established in Canada as elsewhere as a centrepiece of the rituals of remembrance.[1] Closely associated with these formal practices of public commemoration, but secure in its own merit, the poem has endured since as one of the best-known literary works to emerge from the Great War.

'In Flanders Fields' is recognised also as one of the great works of Canadian literature. Its author was born in Guelph, Ontario, which is why the poem serves here as an introduction to a set of symbolic stories about war and identity in the countries of the Commonwealth to which Scottish people emigrated in large numbers. John McCrae's grandfather Thomas McCrae left the family farm in Galloway, Scotland, for a new life in Canada in 1849. The McCraes were of highland stock; family tradition placed an ancestor in the migrations from Kintail which followed the Jacobite defeat at the Battle of Glenshiel in 1719, but it was the inheritance of generations of Lowland farming in Ayrshire and Galloway that bore closer relation to the skills, enterprise and pragmatic outlook through which Thomas McCrae made a success of life in Ontario as stockbreeder and textile mill-owner.[2] His grandson John might be said to have been born not just into the practical, hard-working, strongly Presbyterian culture which emigrants like the McCrae family brought with them to Canada, but also, at a stretch, into the Scottish literary tradition, since the city of Guelph was founded in 1827 by the celebrated novelist and poet John Galt, another Ayrshire man, who complemented his attainments as a writer with a career in colonial land development.

It would be a disservice to Canada, however, to claim John McCrae simply as a Scot. He was, of course, a Canadian by birth, upbringing and outlook. As a self-governing nation of the British empire, the Confederated Dominion of Canada, which was McCrae's home, was not a fully independent state, but it was no colony either. As a soldier, McCrae was a Canadian too. Serving with the Canadian Expeditionary Force in the Great War, he was an officer of the Canadian Army Medical Corps and surgeon of 1st Brigade Canadian Field Artillery. The 400,000 men raised by Canada to fight in France and Flanders were part of the greater British imperial armies, but they were also seen to be representatives of their home nation, a people taking a full and proper part, and shedding its blood in proper order, in a war which was understood to be a fight in defence of liberty and self-determination. In the historiography of Canada, the First World War has commonly been

Above:

Major John McCrae, 1st Brigade Canadian Field Artillery, 1914.

Courtesy of Guelph Museums, McCrae House M1968X.354.1.2

identified, as indeed it was at the time by commentators and propagandists, as a powerful influence which strengthened the popular sense of Canadian national identity. The assumed connection between war and nationhood has been subject to revisionist scrutiny in recent decades, some of it controversial, yet whether that understanding is based on a simplistic reading of history, or, to go further, is merely a reification of wartime propaganda, is in some ways beside the point here. That service and sacrifice in the First World War led Canadians to feel more Canadian is something which many Canadians recognise about their national heritage.[3] A similar idea emerged, and was likewise deliberately fostered, in the popular and public historical cultures of Australia, New Zealand and South Africa, the other main destinations for Scottish migration within the British empire during the nineteenth and early twentieth century. This book's concerns lie at the intersection between this idea of burgeoning nationhood in the Dominions and the different manifestations of Scottish identity and Scottish traditions in war.

John McCrae was both a Canadian soldier and a British subject; he was nevertheless also a Scot. As an artillery officer, he did not serve with one of the many battalions of the wartime Canadian Expeditionary Force which sported Scottish names, Scottish military dress and pipe bands in the manner of the famous Scottish infantry regiments of the British army. But he did have form in this regard. As a 14-year-old, McCrae joined the Guelph Highland Cadet Corps, the oldest school cadet corps in Canada, in which the parade uniform was full highland dress with Royal Stewart tartan kilt and plaid.[4] In this regard the corps mimicked the many part-time units of the Canadian militia which, since 1859, had assumed Scottish military identities almost as a matter of course, as a notable aspect of the overall profile of the constituted defence forces of Canada. This was a cultural practice which was also evident in the reserve military forces of Australia, New Zealand and South Africa, and was to be found too in the defence preparations of Newfoundland, which was a Dominion in its own right prior to confederation with Canada in 1949. The adoption of military identities was complementary to other aspects of Scottish associational culture in the Dominions and was a tribute by emulation to the battlefield successes of the original Scottish regiments which had reflected positively on the profile and reputation of Scotland and her sons throughout the British empire and beyond.

For the young John McCrae studying and teaching medicine in Ontario, the path from highland cadet status led not to one of these Canadian Scottish infantry militia corps, but rather, following in the footsteps of his father, to a commission in the Canadian militia artillery. In December 1899, he interrupted a promising medical career to obtain an appointment as an officer in the artillery of the second contingent of Canadian volunteers sent to bolster British imperial forces in the South African War of 1899–1902. McCrae's experience of campaigning in South Africa reflects another common element in the military and political history of the former British Dominions, the precedent of the war against the Boer republics. For government interests in Canada, the Australia colonies and New Zealand, seeking to balance the relationship between self-government, influence on the cost of imperial defence, and influence on defence policy, there was opportunity in the organisation and provision of volunteers for active service, in having their troops fight alongside British regulars and volunteers as an affirmation of political maturity and responsible government. The same applied to the British community in the South African colonies. Active participation in Britain's wars came at a price in blood and treasure. Dominion and colonial governments could not necessarily assume popular support and a flood of volunteers in response to their policy support for imperial defence.[5] But the bearing of arms in South Africa proved to be a formative experience which set the tone for governmental and popular responses on the outbreak of a major European war in 1914.

Service in the South African War also conferred on the overseas contingents 'a reputation for being natural soldiers in the eyes of the public that sent them'.[6] This idea was based on the notion that life in the former colonies bred a hardy and healthy type, resourceful outdoors-men with skill in riding and other manly endeavours, with born-and-bred physical strength, and a phlegmatic, individualistic attitude to life that made them fearless and indomitable. This may have been a somewhat fanciful interpretation of what daily life in Canada, Australia, New Zealand or South Africa at the turn of the century actually entailed for most of their white inhabitants, relatively few of whom could have claimed any meaningful connection to a notion of the frontier, but it was a powerful ideal. It would come into play again very strongly when Dominion contingents departed for Great War service, providing a myth of national self-image and public expectation to which the awkward reality of experience was required to live up. When confused and costly episodes such as the Gallipoli campaign of 1915 ended in failure, and when the deteriorating conditions of war on the Western Front precluded the possibility of stirring and easy victories for natural soldiers, it was nevertheless through this prism that the battlefield performance of imperial contingents was to be viewed in their own countries. Set-backs were endured, defeats were glorious, mistakes were attributed to others, and the ultimate achievement of British victory was secured with no small thanks to the contribution of the best soldiers at the front, the nationality of which differed depending upon the national point of view.

This kind of partisan response to national performance in military service was not at all the sole preserve of propagandists, press and public opinion in the Dominions. British military culture of course embraced many rivalries which cut across national, regional and local identities, not least between the professional self-regard of the regular soldier and the amateur commitment of the Territorial or volunteer soldier. But if any one part of the British empire had hitherto prided itself on a reputation for being especially and naturally proficient in war, that was surely Scotland. The Scottish military tradition was not merely an expression of national cultural difference, it was also an assertion of the idea of the Scots as a natural warrior race. The Scottish regiments of the British army claimed a heightened reputation as fighters first of all by right of their deeds on battlefields of empire. As an underpinning for that reputation, they identified themselves with an older heritage of the highland clansmen of a partially imagined romantic past, and of the medieval warriors and emigrant mercenary soldiers drawn from all over Scotland who served in the armies of the powers of early modern Europe. Central to all of this was the notion that Scotland, the land itself, highland and lowland, with its rugged and bleak environment and its fierce climate, had bred a hardy type of man who was a warrior by necessity and by inclination.[7] Early twentieth-century myth-making about the soldiers of Canada, Australia and their ilk was not, then, far removed from the assumptions and cultural baggage which Scottish units, of whatever origin, carried with them into the Great War. Just as for the Dominion forces, it was the medium through which the battlefield performance and sacrifice of Scottish units was represented to the home public.[8]

Returning to the precursor of the South African War, responses to British difficulties in the early stages of the conflict set out another marker for the greater conflict which was to follow. When the 'Black Week' of multiple British defeats at the hands of Boer republican forces prompted offers of help for British regular forces from at home and from across the empire, those who stepped forward included volunteers for overseas service who were already serving in part-time 'Scottish' corps locally. Most left their tartan behind when they departed to serve in imperial contingents, but also in evidence in the field in South Africa were constituted Dominion military units of demonstrable Scottish identity, such as the Cape Town Highlanders, 'the oldest kilted regiment in the Southern Hemisphere', formed as a volunteer unit in 1885, and a newly fashioned Scottish unit of international character, the Scottish Horse, which combined mounted troops raised from among the

Scottish community within the South African colonies with contingents of amateur soldiers from Scotland itself and an influx of volunteers of Scottish affinity from Australia.[9] In the Scottish Horse, the idea of an empire-wide community of Scottish citizen soldiers transcended the colonial setting of domestic defence in which the notion had first taken hold. In a state of imperial emergency, fulfilling what they might regard as their patriotic duty to the land of their birth or settlement, men of Scottish descent and affinity would henceforth anticipate the option to serve in 'Scottish' units where the opportunity and inclination arose, but were no less prepared to populate non-Scottish units and arms of service in the expeditionary forces of their homelands.

This observation is the key to a balanced assessment of the Scottish diaspora in the First World War, which must, above all, recognise variety and complexity of experience. What is immediately apparent is that the Dominion Scottish infantry battalions, which were the most overt expressions of the exported Scottish military tradition, were only one part of the story. Among the Dominions, only Canada and South Africa sent Scottish battalions to the Western Front as part of their expeditionary forces, proudly representing their Scottish heritage in the usual combination of distinguishing title, insignia, dress and music; New Zealand, Australia and Newfoundland did not. In the United Kingdom, numbers of Scotsmen of military age resident in the great English cities of London, Liverpool, Newcastle-upon-Tyne and Manchester and their industrial hinterlands, volunteered for locally based Scottish units of the Territorial Force and New Army, but many did otherwise. Scotsmen living in England travelled north to enlist in Scotland, as did numbers of emigrants who chose to return from the United States of America and other parts of the world to join up. Many more enlisted in units and arms of service across the range of the British armed forces which were not designated Scottish. By the latter stages of the war, such were the casualty rates and ongoing exigencies of military organisation, even the home-grown Scottish infantry battalions had seen any original semblance of their cultural coherence become heavily diluted by the drafting of military manpower to where it was most required.

Nevertheless, there is a story to be told. The equations which were made between images of kilted soldiers and a Canadian or South African military identity in cultural and political discourse during, and after, the First World War are so striking as to merit examination. The discrepancy between symbolic representations of this kind and the absence of anything similar in relation to the celebrated 'ANZAC' forces of Australia and New Zealand, also begs exposition.[10] It seems unlikely that the explanation for the difference was entirely cultural.

The Scottish military tradition in citizen soldiering, aligned to the activities of Caledonian societies and other Scottish associations, was as firmly embedded in the civic, professional, commercial and social life of pre-war New Zealand and Australia as it was in South Africa or Canada. Arguably, an outbreak of Scottish-battalion forming, as occurred amidst the raising of the Canadian Expeditionary Force during 1914 and 1915, might just as easily have happened within the Australian and New Zealand expeditionary forces had different institutional circumstances prevailed.

In New Zealand especially, the mobilisation of military manpower proceeded on carefully planned lines, based on a pre-existing system of compulsory military training and service. The nationalisation of reserve military service in New Zealand into the Territorial Force, instituted by the Defence Act of 1909, had discouraged the wholesale transfer of identities from any of the Scottish, or indeed any other volunteer units which had existed prior to the change, and afforded no opportunity for the same to manifest itself in new units formed by rapid expansion of forces when war broke out. No such rapid expansion happened. The New Zealand Expeditionary Force was constructed from cadres of trained soldiers produced by the Territorial Force system, based on careful calculations about how many men the country could reasonably put into the field for a European war and what system and scale of reinforcements would be required to sustain that force at something like full strength through the duration of a long conflict. In this the system proved remarkably successful, although it took the introduction of conscription for overseas service in November 1916 to sustain it through to the end of the war.[11]

In Australia there was likewise in the years leading up to 1914 a national system based on universal compulsory military training. With war declared, the creation of the first contingent of the Australian Imperial Force drew heavily on serving and former Citizen Force members, but not on the existing Citizen Force units, because the Australian government had decided that overseas war service should be entirely voluntary with recruits drawn from across the whole population. Enlistment targets were drawn up based on the different Australian state populations, and while the battalions allotted to each state, and identified by number, might choose to recognise a hereditary connection to pre-existing Citizen Force units, there was no formal relationship between the two.[12] The Scottish kinship claimed between, for example, the 'Victorian Scottish Regiment', properly titled, post-1911, the 52nd (Hobson's Bay) Infantry of the Citizen Force, and the newly created 5th Battalion of the Australian Imperial Force, was a reasonable reflection of the fact that officers and men of the 52nd made a

strong showing in the new overseas service battalion, and indeed supplied its commanding officer. But for all their clannish cohesion, they could not expect to dominate a unit formed from a broader base of former Citizen Force members and fresh volunteers, mostly from Melbourne, in which those of Scottish origin, descent and affinity were outnumbered. While the Scots of the 5th Battalion reportedly held out hope for authorisation of a kilted uniform long after the unit had left Australia's shore, they were to be frustrated in this aspiration, to the relief of the majority of their new comrades.[13] In the 5th, as in other units of the wartime forces of Australia and New Zealand, Scottish identity nevertheless leaked out in a practice beyond the ken and care of official sanction: the creation and maintenance of pipe bands.

The breathing space in which identifiably Scottish infantry battalions emerged in the Canadian Expeditionary Force was a consequence of the quite different approach to mobilisation taken by Canada's Minister of Militia, Colonel Sam Hughes. There were already plans in place to add a division of Canadian troops to imperial forces at the outbreak of war. There were, in fact, two plans, and these were somewhat contradictory. The first, favoured by Canada's director of mobilisation Colonel G. C. W. Gordon-Hall, envisaged making a selection from existing part-time militia units to form the division for overseas service. The second, an earlier proposal drawn up by Gordon-Hall's predecessor Major-General Willoughby Gwatkin, foresaw composite battalions drawn from regions of the country according to population density, which would be assembled, equipped and trained locally before

29

mustering for embarkation. In the event, the unpredictable Hughes decided that neither would meet the requirement in a sufficiently short timespan. At the last minute, in August 1914, he instituted a mobilisation scheme of his own design, conforming to his personal ideal of a citizen volunteer army unhampered by the senior command and staff personnel of the existing militia and permanent force organisations whom he had found to be a hindrance to his initiatives in the past. These supposed obstacles Hughes simply bypassed as he sent telegrams to the commanding officers of every militia battalion in the country inviting them to recruit as many volunteers as possible, organise them into one or two companies and bring them to Valcartier, Quebec, to a camp yet to be built, where the Canadian Expeditionary Force would be assembled, organised and trained.[14]

The response was enthusiastic, and the results predictably confused. Many more men arrived at Valcartier than the 25,000 that were required. Little training of practical value could be conducted while the assembled force went through a sequence of reorganisations, with battalions and higher formations being formed and reformed and officers jockeying for position in the new overseas force. Later, speaking in 1916, Hughes affirmed to the Canadian parliament that his mobilisation plan had sought above all to capitalise on the spirit of patriotic enthusiasm which was present among the early volunteers, and acknowledged that the plan was as much concerned with tapping into the urgency of this crusading spirit as it was with practical measures. He described his rather traditional approach to recruiting as 'really a call to arms, like the fiery cross passing through the highlands of Scotland, or the mountains of Ireland in former days'.[15] Small wonder then, that in this first rush to the colours, and in the subsequent expansion of the force to provide the first two contingents of the Canadian Expeditionary Force, the freedom given to local militia battalion commanders and prominent private citizens to raise new battalions at their own behest brought forth fully formed, fully staffed infantry battalions with titles, distinguishing insignia and uniforms of their own choosing. Unsurprisingly, given the emigrant profile of Canada, a healthy proportion of these, from areas of especially strong Scottish settlement, or where commanding officers or local notables had a personal affinity for things Scottish, sported distinctively Scottish military identities.

The first Canadian contingent was oversubscribed by no fewer than 150 battalions, and the confusion which this unleashed at Valcartier was not the end of the problem. In contrast to the planned system of reinforcements pioneered in New Zealand, Canadian recruitment continued unchecked in the Sam Hughes vein. Ever more men were offered for second and third overseas contingents which ultimately increased the Canadian presence at the front from two to five divisions, in the form of more and more new battalions. Two especial problems arose. The new battalions each carried a full complement of officers, and expected to serve and fight together. When it became apparent that this was not going to be possible for all of them, and when it transpired that, in order to replace casualties in units already overseas, officers and men were going to be sent to other battalions, there was unhappiness in the ranks and resistance from commanding officers.[16] Relatively few of the new Scottish battalions, like many of the other battalions raised for overseas service, departed Canada under their original title and organisational composition. Their personnel were instead drafted into other units, or became reserve battalions in England feeding recruits to front-line units. More critically, for a time, men sorely needed on the Western Front were held up in Canada while their officers dallied and lobbied Hughes and his staff, pressing for their units to be kept together. It was only the demand for a more rational system of reinforcement, occasioned by the unsentimental realities of casualty rates in late 1914 and 1915, which meant there were not even more Canadian-Scottish battalions in action on the Western Front. However, a sufficient number made it intact through all the improvisations and reorganisations to constitute a strong Scottish presence in the Canadian Corps which, in the last two years of the war, made a considerable reputation for itself as a highly capable fighting formation. Of the 69 battalions which existed at some stage as part of the operational Canadian Corps in France and Flanders and in the United Kingdom, 11 had Scottish titles.

South Africa's manpower contribution to the war in Europe was necessarily more modest, but within it the Scottish element was if anything more conspicuous. The South African Infantry Brigade of volunteers which was assembled at Pochefstroom in 1915 was four battalions strong, and one of these, the 4th South African Infantry, unofficially titled 'the South African Scottish', mustered with a strong showing from the ranks of pre-war Union Defence Force part-time units the Transvaal Scottish of Johannesburg and the Cape Town Highlanders and Duke of Edinburgh's Rifles of Cape Town. The raising of the Brigade was, as with Canada, something of an improvisation and its recruitment profile and organisation were dictated by the unique circumstances of the country's recent history. The Union of South Africa was a British Dominion of only four years standing, fashioned from four former colonies, two of them the recently conquered former Boer republics. The Union's domestic politics hinged on the fragile relationship between the British and Afrikaner identities of the white populations which dominated the government of the country. The outbreak of a European war in 1914 interrupted a fraught process of post-war reconstruction still raw in political, cultural and economic terms.

In the years between the Boer surrender and the outbreak of the Great War, the British-Afrikaner stress line had been overlaid by industrial disputes within the mining industry and by pressure and protest among the majority African and Asian populations pushing against their subservient economic and political status. The Union government was led by two former Boer republican generals, Louis Botha and Jan Christian Smuts, who were reconciled and committed to their country's future as part of the British empire. Not all of their Afrikaner compatriots were similarly convinced and Botha's government had to exercise caution in demanding military service in Europe on behalf of the British Crown. South Africa's war effort commenced with the invasion of neighbouring German South-West Africa (Namibia), an incursion which provoked the Afrikaner Rebellion amongst German-sympathising Boers serving with Union Defence Force troops poised on the border. The rebellion quickly fizzled out, attracting only hardline Afrikaner active support, but the conquest of German South-West Africa which followed failed to overshadow entirely this demonstration of lingering internal division. Fighting for Britain remained a hard sell in parts of South Africa. The despatch of volunteers to supplement British and Indian forces in the protracted campaign in German East Africa (Tanzania), which was stepped up by Smuts from mid-1914, failed to provide the rousing victory which the pro-empire Union government required to vindicate its policy of imperial co-operation.

In support of these military ventures on African soil, the government could at least make an appeal across the white population on the basis that the defensive and territorial expansion interests of South Africa were in play, as well as the overall fate of the British empire. But the greater ambition was to maximise South Africa's part in the war and so assert its nationhood at the conference table of empire in the future. In seeking to make their aspiration a reality, Botha and Smuts had limited room for manoeuvre. Care was required in managing the traction gained by the new opposition Afrikaner National Party in rejecting the obligation to fight as a divisive and inappropriate distraction from domestic political and economic challenges, including its concerns over the restiveness of the black majority. That is not to say that there was an absence of patriotic enthusiasm for European war service in the country – far from it. There were, from the outset, displays of loyal support for a South African war effort across the country and agitation that it should be increased. The volunteers for the South African Overseas Expeditionary Force who assembled at Potchefstroom from 1915, albeit prominently urban middle class and of British descent, included many Afrikaners.[17] African and Asian organisations, representing black and coloured populations who were denied the status of combatants and the implications of full citizenship which this carried, also mobilised manpower for overseas war service in auxiliary and labour roles, in the expectation of seeing future reward for their loyalty and participation.

Such were the contentions around the Union's military contribution to the war, the government was compelled to define and deliver the Overseas Expeditionary Force as British imperial troops, specifically not as part of the constituted forces of the Union of South Africa. The niceties of this accommodation might have seemed an irrelevance, had it not meant that the overseas volunteers therefore received British rates of daily pay substantially below the equivalent for South Africa's own Union troops in German South-West and East Africa. This discrepancy was to rankle with the volunteers for years, especially when they came into contact with other Dominion troops on the Western Front and discovered the extent of their own relative poverty.[18] Content or not, the South African Brigade dispatched to Europe at the end of 1915 was the reflection of one partial idea of what South Africa represented, with its recruitment make-up – white, middle class, mostly British descended or immigrant loyalist volunteers, many of them cadet-trained. The black African and mixed race auxiliaries of the South African Native Labour Corps, the Cape Coloured Labour Battalion and other such formations, also on the British pay-roll, were deployed separately on labour and transport duties, mainly in northern French ports, under white South African officers and British direction.[19]

Within the South African Brigade, hastily recruited and organised, there was again, as in Canada, the opportunity for pre-existing cultural identities and affinities to find expression. The South African Scottish, with its background in the Scottish expatriate communities, volunteer regiments and Caledonian societies of Johannesburg and Cape Town, made itself readily distinguishable. Something of a late starter, its arrival on the Western Front was further postponed by its despatch from England to the Senussi campaign in north Africa. By the time its job there was done and the Brigade disembarked for the first time in France, at Marseilles, it was April 1916. The men of the South African Scottish had swapped their tropical helmets worn in the north African desert for the khaki 'Tam o' Shanter' bonnets worn by Scottish infantry-men, were sporting the Murray of Atholl tartan kilts which they had been issued at Bordon Camp in Hampshire in November 1915 and, led through the streets by the pipe and drums, playing instruments received as a gift from a patriotic well-wisher in Johannesburg, they created quite a stir locally in their ceremonial debut on French soil.[20]

The extent to which Scottish military identity transcended the 4th South African Infantry and attached itself to the South African Brigade as a whole is a phenomenon which has attracted the interest and comment of South African historians. The Scottish connection, described by one commentator as 'a contagious kind of diaspora "Scottishness"', complemented the identity and coherence of the whole Brigade, the majority of which wore the uniform of conventional British infantry.[21] As in the Canadian context, the factors promoting this development did not lie solely in the cultural arena. The ascendancy of Scottish identity also owed something to the happenstance which saw the South Africans deployed for operational service on the Western Front as one of the constituent brigades of 9th (Scottish) Division, a formation which was based on 'New Army' infantry battalions of war-service volunteers recruited in Scotland. There was no pan-Caledonian sentiment involved in the initiation of this relationship; the arrival of the South Africans proceeded from the need to reorganise 9th (Scottish) Division in March 1916, a requirement which reflected poor planning for reinforcements, poor British planning in this instance, in the original mobilisation. More battalions had been raised in Scotland than it was possible to sustain with fresh volunteer manpower over months and years. The arrival of the South Africans into the division's new order of battle aroused curiosity among their Scottish comrades at first, and the divisional commander and his staff noted the strength, stature and health of the new arrivals, indication that the Dominion self-image of superior physique and constitution had some evidential basis.[22]

Similarly, the pragmatic demands of war mobilisation, rather than a purely cultural impetus, accounted for the timing and context in which Scottish units formed in English cities found their way to the Western Front. Battalions of the London Scottish and Liverpool Scottish led the way. These battalions were part of the Territorial Force of part-time, trained volunteers which had been established in 1908 by reorganising the former 'Volunteer Battalions' associated with regular regiments. The 1st Battalion London Scottish attained the distinction of being the first Territorial battalion to see action on the Western Front, making an early name for itself, and an impressive debut for the Territorial Force as a whole, in a moment of crisis on Hallowe'en 1914, advancing successfully to consolidate the British hold on Messines Ridge against a German attack. Unlike the Scottish battalions from the Dominions, these volunteers of London and Liverpool arrived in France and Flanders in the later months of 1914 in the formed units which they had joined before hostilities broke out. By virtue of their members volunteering *en masse* for overseas service, they, like other British Territorial units, stayed ahead of new battalions being raised by direct

Above:

Men of the Liverpool
Scottish on the beach at
Blackpool, 1915.

© National Museums
Scotland

enlistment of volunteers. The latter were the 'New Armies' raised at the urging of Secretary of State for War Lord Kitchener, and were the British equivalent to the recruiting enterprises in Canada and South Africa creating expeditionary forces from scratch.

The pre-war part-timers and fresh volunteers of the London and Liverpool Scottish were designated as Territorial battalions of English regiments: the County of London Regiment and the King's (Liverpool) Regiment respectively. They could lay claim to unit ancestries which, allowing for interruptions, ran back over decades to the volunteer rifle companies formed by the Scottish professional and commercial classes in their cities in 1859. The ancestry went further back in the case of London, where two Scottish units had formed part of the array of London volunteer companies during the Napoleonic wars. Furthermore, both the London Scottish and Liverpool Scottish had sent active service companies of volunteers to the South African War in 1900, with elements from each unit serving in companies attached to the regular infantry battalions of the Gordon Highlanders. Bolstered though they were in 1914 by an influx of new recruits for war service, the London and Liverpool Scottish maintained their middle-class volunteer ethos on departure to the Western Front. With officers and other ranks sharing similar social backgrounds as university, professional and commercial men, they were defined as much by class as by the Scottish affinity they professed.[23]

The genesis of the Scottish contingents recruited around Newcastle-upon-Tyne, Manchester and Salford was, institutionally, quite different. As New Army recruits enlisted during the flood of volunteering in Britain in the summer and autumn of 1914, their soldiers were part of that rush to the colours which occurred independently of the pre-war provisions of the Territorial Force system. On his appointment as Secretary for War on the day after the British declaration of war, Lord Kitchener foresaw a long conflict and the need, if Britain was to prevail in it, to do much more than reinforce the regular and Territorial soldiers of the British Expeditionary Force being despatched to France and Flanders. His goal was to enlarge the British army in the field significantly, to which end some three million volunteers were enlisted before conscription was introduced in January 1916. One recruiting tactic adopted to fill these 'Kitchener Battalions', principally in urban areas, was the proffering of the guaranteed opportunity to serve with friends and workplace colleagues in what were known as the 'Pals Battalions'. The Scottish recruiting efforts in Newcastle and Manchester may be viewed as one manifestation of this idea.

Like London and Liverpool, both of these northern cities had their business networks of middle-class Scots, and their Caledonian and St Andrew's societies to go with them, but only Newcastle had produced a Scottish volunteer company in peacetime, and that had lasted only a few years beyond its inception in 1859. Plans had been hatched in 1900 among prominent Scottish citizens of Newcastle-upon-Tyne to revive the idea for the South African War but, unlike in Liverpool where the dormant Liverpool Scottish was reactivated, these had not come to fruition on Tyneside. Without any existing cadre upon which to expand, no fewer than four New Army battalions were raised from among the Scots of Tyneside by January 1915, a full infantry brigade over 5000 men strong, from what amounted to a standing start; this was something of a recruiting phenomenon, especially since the combined recruiting committees of Tyneside, which included Tyneside Irish and 'Commercial' battalions in addition to the Scottish, raised around 15,000 men in total.[24] Scots were by no means the biggest immigrant community in the north-east of England. There was a healthy showing of 'affinity Scots', and those of no previous Scottish inclination whatsoever, in the ranks of the Tyneside Scottish which set up no origin or ancestry stipulation for recruits.[25] With this scale of enlistment, and whether or not recruits shared impeccable Scottish heritage, the Tyneside Scottish battalions reflected a social profile rather different from the élite volunteer unit heritage of their London and Liverpool counterparts, being recruited largely from workers in the coal-mining, shipbuilding and other heavy industries of Tyneside. In common with established practice in the Territorial Force and New Armies, the battalions of the Tyneside Scottish Brigade were designated battalions of the local regular regiment, in this case becoming service battalions of the Northumberland Fusiliers.

The Manchester contingent was raised in similar organisational circumstances, but at rather a more modest scale. The prominent Scottish citizens of Manchester could not draw on a Scotland-derived population in the north-west to quite the same extent as any of their three municipal counterparts. Nevertheless, in the face of intense competition from rival local recruiting committees, they managed to amass somewhere in the region of 500 men.[26] This was not a sufficient number to form a battalion in its own right, and the notion of contributing a battalion to be part of the New Army complement of the Manchester Regiment did not come to pass. Instead the Manchester Scottish recruiting committee exercised the option of offering their enlisted men to a Scottish New Army battalion at that time forming in Edinburgh. By this route, the 'Manchester Scottish' became part of the strength of 15th (Service) Battalion Royal Scots, which had been recruiting in its own right as a new City of Edinburgh volunteer battalion.

Neither the 15th Battalion Royal Scots nor the Tyneside Scottish Brigade was allocated to one of the British army's Scottish infantry divisions. This was not at all an unusual situation for Scottish infantry battalions of any description, which as well as being concentrated in the Territorial and New Army divisions carrying 'Scottish', 'Highland' or 'Lowland' designations, were scattered throughout British fighting formations. The Scots of Tyneside and Manchester were placed instead in the 34th Division, a formation characterised by its strong complement of Pals battalions. With the added strength of the New Armies, British forces made ready for a major offensive on the Somme in the summer of 1916. This placed these new Anglo-Scottish battalions in the assault on La Boiselle on 1st July, the infamous first day of the battle of the Somme, and so into a baptism of fire which took a toll of casualties disastrous even by the established standards of warfare on the Western Front.

The New Armies had much in common with the forces raised in the British Dominions. With only a very limited complement of professional and experienced officers to go round, they were in the main composed of amateur soldiers. They had to find their feet, individually and collectively, and make their way in the complex and challenging conditions of massively destructive industrial mass warfare with little preparation and limited opportunity for concerted training. As they learned how to be soldiers, and how to fight the war, they did so under the direction of a high command struggling to overcome the technological and tactical problems which war at this scale presented. The

'lions led by donkeys' school of First World War historiography, popular during the 1960s and 1970s, laid the blame for the war's shocking
casualty rate at the door of incompetence, mismanagement and lack of
imagination on the part of British high command. This view has largely
been superseded, in academic military history circles at least, by more
balanced assessments of how strategy, tactics and training were over-
hauled, albeit through a costly process of trial and error in which
incompetence was a factor, enabling the ultimate British victory in
1918 by fighting design as well as through enemy exhaustion.[27]

The German army was defeated in the field in the summer and
autumn of 1918, and one factor behind the Allied victory was the
uneven but growing competence of British fighting formations,
including those drawn from Canada, Australia, New Zealand and
South Africa. The 'lions led by donkeys' interpretation found traction
in these countries also, in part because it suited perfectly the national
foundation narratives based on the prowess and heroism of Commonwealth soldiers. These scenarios of popular memory had to encompass
heavy losses and defeats – as for the Anzac forces at Gallipoli – as well
as the ultimate victory. The laying of blame exclusively at the door of
British general officers was an understandable response to a costly war
which was directed from the imperial centre. But in recent decades, and
not without public controversy, historians in these Commonwealth
countries have similarly begun to question these kinds of assumptions,
scrutinising national self-image and examining how the battlefield
performance of their expeditionary forces evolved and progressed,
apportioning credit and blame where it was due among higher command, divisional, and brigade commanders and fighting units of their
own nationalities.[28]

And yet there is no avoiding a reckoning with the catastrophic loss
of life which persists in any overview of the First World War, even in a
book such as this one concerned with developments in military and
national identities rather than with the course and conduct of the war
itself. To read, by way of example, the story of the South African
Brigade on the Western Front, is to be reminded of the human toll taken
by repeated exposure to battle in that war. The action at Delville Wood
in July 1916, in which the South Africans endured days under devas-
tating assault and bombardment, was singled out for public remembrance in South Africa on account of the harrowing cost in lives taken,
but this was merely one occasion on which the Brigade was all but
destroyed and had to be rebuilt with fresh recruits. Later in 1916, still
on the Somme, in attacking the heavily defended spur known as the
Butte de Warlencourt; again in April 1917 at the village of Fampoux
during the British Arras offensive; and again, in the British retreat of

March 1918, back on the Somme once more, in an isolated stand at Marrières Wood which ended in surrender, but which prevented a potentially disastrous enemy breakthrough – the South Africans went through the mill until only a small remnant was left standing.

When Canadian John McCrae's 'In Flanders Field' spoke for the dead, exhorting the living to carry on the fight, he spoke from the thick of it and without the bitterness of long hindsight. He expressed similar sentiments later in the war in 'The Anxious Dead', written while he was serving at No. 3 Canadian General Hospital Boulogne, and published in September 1917. But McCrae's colleagues and friends had noticed a change in his temperament. Months and years of receiving and treating the wounded, as well as the mental and physical strain of his own battle experiences and mounting illness, wore him down. McCrae believed, and believed solemnly, in the necessity of prosecuting the war, but he found little glory amidst the reality of battle, and little of grand heroic sentiment in sacrifice. The excitement and patriotism for empire and for home nation which characterised the mobilisation of military man-power in the Dominions in 1914 must have seemed increasingly distant notions to men, like McCrae, who in the ensuing years had learned first-hand what industrialised war was all about. Seen from the perspective of influential political and social constituencies in the British Dominions in 1914, the prospect of participation, action and victory was perceived as an opportunity to assert mature nationhood. Few among these constituencies at that time could have anticipated the price that ultimately would have to be paid for that victory.

In the end the assertions of national unity, and of national coming of age, were based on sacrifice, on the shedding of blood, as much as on the grounds of victory, and were predictable cultural and political responses to the trauma of collective loss and private grief on a scale previously unimagined. It was only to be expected that the leaders of Dominion societies should continue to seek meaning and redemption from their countries' part in the chaos and destruction that had been unleashed. No one was hiding from the realisation that the Great War had been fought at catastrophic cost, but this was not to lose sight of the fact that the war had been won in the end, and that the contribution of the British Dominions was an acknowledged factor in that victory. One physical manifestation of this response was the erection of nation-ally designated war memorials at the battlefield sites of greatest national resonance. For the South Africans this was Delville Wood. For the Canadians it was Vimy Ridge, where in April 1917 the Canadian Corps had performed its greatest collective military feat and made its most concentrated sacrifice. For the Dominion of Newfoundland the distinctive bronze caribou memorial at Beaumont Hamel marked the site of 1st Battalion Newfoundland Regiment's costly attack on the first day of the Battle of the Somme. The battlefield at Beaumont Hamel was sacred ground shared with other monuments, including the bronze figure commemorating Scotland's own 51st (Highland) Division. The caribou represented an assertion of Newfoundland nationhood embodied by equality of sacrifice on this blood-soaked ground.[29] For New Zealanders and Australians the feeling was expressed in the memorials and cemeteries built in the immediate post-war years around and above 'Anzac Cove' on the Gallipoli peninsula, which, on the territory of Turkey, victor in the campaign but defeated in the war, was symbolically claimed as national sovereign space.[30] Between allies, the claim went beyond the symbolic. Walter Allward's Canadian memorial at Vimy Ridge, unveiled in 1936, was built on 250 acres of the former battlefield which had been formally ceded by France to Canada in 1922. Each of the Dominion governments made purchases and transfer agreements with landowners and government bodies in France in order to secure permanent title to those devastated landscapes which were the scenes of their most memorable and most catastrophic days.

Similar conviction was expressed through the construction of war memorials on Dominion home soil. Just as in communities across Great Britain, simple local memorials were raised to honour the dead whose graves, if they had any, lay on foreign battlefields. These sites of community commemoration were primarily public expressions of private mourning. They were complemented by grander schemes of homage

Below:

'The Cheerful Scottie' – Canadian official photograph, Battle of Vimy Ridge, April 1917.

CWM 19920044-875 George Metcalf Archival Collection © Canadian War Museum

and pride at municipal, provincial and state level, as in the creation of the Auckland War Memorial and Museum in New Zealand's most populous city. But in initiating and supporting these plans for national war memorial schemes, Dominion élites also aspired to proclaim national unity, societal maturity, and parity with the old country in sacrifice and the achievement of victory. While the imperial capital contented itself with the classical simplicity and universality of Sir Edwin Lutyens' Cenotaph in Whitehall, Dominion designs were more assertive. South Africa's delicate domestic politics complicated the picture, and the very remoteness of Herbert Baker's Delville Wood South African National Memorial in France, far away from the locus of tension between British and Afrikaner conceptions of national heritage, was probably an advantage to its creators and supporters; but smaller replica monuments, likewise stressing the unity of the two white races, were nevertheless installed at three prominent sites in South Africa.[31] The Canadian National War Memorial in Ottawa's Confederation Square was long in the making. English sculptor Vernon March's 'The Response', unveiled in 1939, enshrined a group of 22 bronze figures from all services to represent the Canadian nation in arms in its entirety, with one kilted and Lewis-gun-carrying infantryman prominent. Its memorial function complemented a long-standing aspiration to give the city of Ottawa the kind of ceremonial space that a new nation might expect from its capital.[32]

The New Zealand National War Memorial in Wellington, incorporating a 49-bell carillon, was formally opened on 'Anzac Day', 25 April 1932. The original conception as expressed by the National War Memorial Committee in 1919 was for a monument which would 'be of immense influence in the formation of New Zealand national character'.[33] The adoption of the anniversary of the first landings at Anzac Cove, Gallipoli, as a national day of commemoration was an indicator that the rituals of remembrance for New Zealanders lay within a distinctive national narrative as well as within the broader imperial context, albeit one shared, not always altogether comfortably, with their Australian neighbours.[34] As will be explored in a later chapter, Australian governmental aspirations for national commemoration kept pace with the British government's scheme of commemoration and preservation of public record and memory which became London's Imperial War Museum. The Australian War Memorial, conceived as early as 1917, and eventually opened in Canberra on 11 November 1941, was simultaneously a memorial monument, national museum with collections intended to venerate the fallen and the veterans, and a sombre celebration, but a celebration none the less, of what it meant to be an Australian in the aftermath of the Great War.[35]

To stress the significance of these tributes in stone is not necessarily
to accept their uncomplicated representations of national unity. The
Dominions had experienced tensions and internal divisions during the
war years. Australia and Canada had seen protests over proposals to
introduce conscription, rejected by plebiscite in the former. Contesting
identities, not only in South Africa but also, for example, in the case of
the French Canadians and among Irish immigrants to Australia, was
a factor influencing reticence over, and in some instances outright
opposition to, participation in the imperial war effort.[36] But these were
minority views, and not, naturally, the memories which Dominion
political élites wished to enshrine. The contributions of aboriginal
populations to national war efforts, a matter of considerable political
import in negotiating their future status, were likewise incorporated in
the representations of unitary nationhood.

As assertive as any of these monuments, more assertive perhaps,
was the Scottish National War Memorial opened in Edinburgh Castle in
1927. In Scotland too, a group of prominent figures from the military
and social establishment saw as their duty the conception and construction of a place of homage to Scotland's war dead, where loss could be
commemorated in national cultural terms. There was no implicit
tension between the idea of a definitively Scottish sacrifice and the
assimilation of this experience into the wider British and imperial
rituals of remembrance. And yet the symbolism of the memorial in
Edinburgh Castle spoke of historic nationhood in ways that the

Cenotaph in London, and indeed equivalent structures raised in Cardiff for the war dead of Wales, and in Dublin for the fallen of Ireland, did not. In its home-grown architecture and artistry, and, especially, in its privileging of the identities of the Scottish regiments in the organisation and decoration of the 'Hall of Honour' within, the Memorial referenced not only the loss of Scottish lives, individually named, but also the honour and reputation of the collective military tradition which, by its very existence and location on the highpoint of national sacred space, it interpreted as a defining element of Scottish heritage. The terminology of 'Lowlander' and 'Highlander', the names of the old regiments, written large in the memorial, with their heraldry and deeds carved in stone, were points of honour in themselves. In the conception of the Scottish National War Memorial, Scottish dead had to be honoured in Scottish terms, and there was a ready-made symbolic language through which this could be expressed. In this, the migrant Scots of the British Dominions would not be forgotten.

For the living, as for the dead, and for the Dominion Scottish as for the home-grown Scots, much of the mystique of military, or militaristic, Scotland was conveyed in outward display. The kilt, the distinctive headgear (whether of 'glengarry' or 'Tam o' Shanter' variety), the heraldic differentiation in cap badges and other insignia, and, adding sound to the spectacle, the martial music of the bagpipes, made up the panoply. This was a combination which was instantly recognisable to friend and foe alike. For the wearer it offered a sense of belonging, the individual embraced into a prestigious tradition older, and stronger than himself alone, and thereby a source of confidence and motivation for men required to fight and possibly to die. As a message for those fighting on the same side, it was a statement of pride and a challenge. Rivalry within and between armies is a perennial and near-universal aspect of military organisational culture; the Scottish image was one means, amongst the many which the practice of war has produced, of impressing others, proclaiming toughness, claiming élite status and competing for glory. The battlefield performance of Scottish regiments was something to be measured against. As a message to the enemy, it was a chest-beating display of aggression and defiance. There was satisfaction to be had in being recognised as Scottish, and respected, or preferably feared, for it. The belief that German military intelligence had marked out one Scottish formation on the Western Front, the 51st (Highland) Division, as *berühmte* ('renowned' or 'formidable'), was accordingly the source of much satisfaction. This unsubstantiated report subsequently became something of a shibboleth of the Scottish military tradition, although it might constitute nothing more than lore.[37]

The abiding appeal of the Scottish martial image lay in its being simultaneously flamboyant and aggressive. In the khaki-clad anonymity of industrial-scale warfare, the colourful assertiveness of tartan was endowed with heroic qualities of war-making. In 20th century warfare this might have been some distance removed from contemporary realities – the kilt was no practical help and was something of a hindrance in trench warfare – but it was not out of place. Military culture and tradition was part of the individual and collective psychological arsenal of the soldier. Men who had to exist with hardship and fear, who lived at the mercy of a war machine so much bigger than anything they as individuals could do much to impact upon, and who had to face up to the possibility of mutilation or annihilation by these forces beyond their control, most likely by artillery, an enemy they could not see, naturally sought some vestiges of the more human scale of warfare, and of the kudos of being a warrior.[38] The Scottish image was not only a form of boasting, it was an expression of exaggerated masculinity. The Gaelic warrior culture to which, in certain aspects, it harked back was one in which masculine accomplishment, recognition of male prowess, and beauty found in physical strength, was expressed without reserve. Much in military culture after all is a manifestation of male display and intended, alongside its more combative functions, to draw the admiration of women. So, for the young volunteers of Nova Scotia, lining up to join the Canadian Expeditionary Force, the cap badge motto chosen for their new battalion was the Gaelic '*Siol na fear fearail*', 'the breed of manly men'. Settlement patterns in Nova Scotia entailed an especially close identification with Gaelic Scotland, but their motto might stand here for the phenomenon of the Scottish military tradition. Perhaps for this reason, for the flamboyance of its masculine assertion, the Scottish warrior image has always been highly vulnerable to lampoon, but the one place where it was in no way comical was on the field of battle. In the ultimate test of men, the sense of Scottish difference was culturally sanctioned, and the effect was widely admired.[39]

Even so, sentiments such as these were rarely expressed directly or verbally. These were assumptions and assertions which were conveyed through symbolism, which is why the chapters which follow use the medium of material culture to explore the experiences of Commonwealth Scots in the Great War. Each chapter takes as its starting point an artefact, chosen for its symbolic significance, which is preserved and treasured in a public collection in its country of origin, and which was brought to Scotland to form the spine of the *Common Cause*

Below:

Maple-leaf shaped glengarry badge of the 85th Canadian Infantry Battalion (Nova Scotia Highlanders) with Gaelic motto.

© National Museums Scotland

44

centenary exhibition at the National Museum of Scotland from July to October 2014. An artefact from the collections of National Museums Scotland, which encompass the national military collections and the material culture of the Scottish diaspora, continues the story. Precious objects, the stories they represent, and the values invested in them, offer a means of investigating that intangible and complex element of collective human behaviour and motivation, identity. These objects were selected for this book, and as the centrepieces of the exhibition which it accompanies, to represent, above all, the plurality of identities which migrant Scots and their descendants took to war. Tartan and bagpipes feature among them, as of course they would. In emulating the celebrated Scottish regiments of the British army, pre-war Dominion Scottish units had gone to great lengths to procure the requisite uniform, adopting dress distinctions and traditions of the Scottish regiments with which they chose to associate themselves, in many cases ordering tartan, sporrans and other impedimenta direct from source in Scotland or benefiting from issue of existing army supplies. In the wartime units of Canada and South Africa, similar trouble and expense was undertaken to ensure that Scottish identity was promulgated as far as possible, with kilts, bonnets and pipers on the battalion strength. The piping tradition, indeed, is the one area in which traditional Scottish military culture emerged right across the expeditionary forces of the British Dominions, including Australia and New Zealand, whether officially sanctioned or privately promoted.

But the range of artefacts presented in the following chapters is far wider. As we have seen, the Scots of what is now the Commonwealth were just as much engaged with new forms of identity and new brands of national military culture, more indeed, as they were with the perpetuation of the old ones. These nascent military cultures evolved national military symbols of their own, and some of these are represented here in relation to the diaspora Scots who came under their influence and who adopted them as their own. And all of these symbolic expressions were related to the broader British imperial culture of war in which they evolved. Whether as markers of difference or not, they were part of that common inheritance, and were dedicated in 1914 to the common cause of defending British imperial hegemony and the freedoms and values it was believed to represent.

Identity is a subtle, subjective matter, and caveats are always required when addressing the collective consciousness. The multitudes who volunteered or who were conscripted for war service had more pressing individual concerns than ruminations over whether and how they could simultaneously be Scottish and Canadian, or could be Australian and British, and so on. The stories of a very small selection of these men will be represented in what follows, so that in their humanity and individuality, like John McCrae, they might stand for many more. They all had families and comrades and their own futures to worry about. They had an enemy to encounter and the chances of their personal survival to reckon with. As they boarded troopships and ferries to the theatres of war, many would have carried within them anxiety over not knowing how they would behave at the moment of battle, and few can have been immune to the impulse to acquit themselves honourably in the eyes of their fellows and of posterity, come what may. At a distance of one hundred years on from 1914, we cannot presume to speak for them. We might instead merely express the hope that, at the individual level, knowing a part of them was Scottish, with all that being Scottish was meant to embody for men going to war, was in some small way a source of sustenance in the trials which awaited.

Notes

1 Harding 2001, p. 121.
2 Graves 1997, p. 1–7.
3 For a comparative discussion of this idea, see Jeff Keshen, 'The Great War as nation builder in Canada and Australia' in Busch (ed.) 2003, pp. 3–26.
4 A Highland Cadet Corps uniform of c.1898 is preserved in the collection of Guelph Museums, acc. no. 1975.35.1.8.
5 On controversy in Australia over provision of support for the war in South Africa, see Grey 1999, p. 52–3.
6 Pugsley 2004, p. 38.
7 On the evolution of the Scottish military tradition, see Edward Spiers 'Introduction' in Spiers et al. 2012, pp. 1–38. See also Allan and Carswell 2004, p. 15–44.
8 On the place of Scottish highlanders in the imperial discourse of 'martial races', see Streets 2004, pp. 179–82.
9 Orpen 1986, p. 1; Mackenzie with Dalziel 2007, pp. 255–6.
10 The ANZAC 'Australian and New Zealand Army Corps' was, technically, a British army corps formed in April 1915 from Australian Imperial Force and New Zealand Expeditionary Force contingents assembled in Egypt prior to re-embarkation for the Gallipoli campaign.
11 Pugsley 2004, pp. 51–70.
12 Grey 1999, pp. 73–86.
13 Speed 1988, pp. 20–4.
14 For an examination of the politics and organisation of Canadian mobilisation planning, see Harris 1988, pp. 94–109. The problems associated with Hughes' decisions were recognised at the time and were later acknowledged in the official history, Nicholson 1962, pp. 14–62.
15 Quoted in Haycock 1986, p. 181.
16 Harris 1988, p. 109.
17 Nasson 2007, pp. 123–5.
18 Ibid., pp. 95 and 126.
19 Wineguard 2012, pp. 165–84.
20 Digby 1993, pp. 82–8.
21 Bill Nasson, 'Delville Wood and South African Great War commemoration', English Historical Review 119, 480, February 2004, pp. 57–86. See also Jonathan Hyslop, 'Cape Town Highlanders, Transvaal Scottish: "military Scottishness" and social power in nineteenth and twentieth century South Africa', South African Historical Journal 47 (1), 2002, pp. 96–114.
22 Ewing 1921, pp. 81–2.
23 McCartney 2005, pp. 19–21.
24 Stewart and Sheen 1999, pp. 25–45.
25 Beckett and Simpson (eds) 1985, p. 106.
26 Dowson 2000, pp. 1–12.
27 Sheffield 2001, pp. 1–20. On the British historiography of the First World War, see also Bond 2002.
28 A useful example is Andrews 1993.
29 Paul Gough, 'Sites in the imagination: the Beaumont Hamel Newfoundland Memorial on the Somme', Cultural Geographies 11, 2004, pp. 235–58.
30 John McQuilton, 'Gallipoli as contested commemorative space', in Macleod (ed.) 2012, pp. 150–8.
31 Bill Nasson, 'Delville Wood and South African Great War commemoration', English Historical Review 119, 480, February 2004, pp. 57–86.
32 David L. A. Gordon and Brian S. Osbourne, 'Constructing national identity in Canada's capital, 1900–2000: Confederation Square and the National War Memorial', Journal of Historical Geography 30, 2004, pp. 618–42.
33 Maclean and Phillips 1990, pp. 119–22.
34 In the Anzac Cove landings of 25 April 1915, Australian troops predominated in the fighting of that first day. While the outstanding symbolic moment of New Zealand endeavour sacrifice came later in the campaign, at Chunuk Bair on 8 August, this did not prevent the combined Anzac commemorative calendar taking hold in New Zealand. Pugsley 1998, pp. 344–57.
35 Inglis assisted by Brazier 1998, pp. 333–47.
36 Patrick A. Dutil, 'Against isolationism: Napoléon Belcourt, French Canada and 'La grand guerre', in MacKenzie (ed.) 2005, pp. 96–137, and Andrews 1993, pp. 126–8.
37 The matter was referred to in the divisional history and repeated in other sources. Bewsher 1921, p. 410.
38 Stephenson 2012, p. 205.
39 Heather Streets, 'Identity in the highland regiments in the nineteenth century: soldier, region, nation', in Murdoch and Mackillop (eds), pp. 213–36.

Bibliography

Allan, Stuart and Allan Carswell 2004. *The Thin Red Line: War, Empire and Visions of Scotland* (Edinburgh: National Museums Scotland).

Andrews, E. M. 1993. *The Anzac Illusion: Anglo-Australian Relations during World War I* (Cambridge).

Beckett, Ian and Keith Simpson (eds) 1985. *A Nation in Arms. A Social Study of the British Army in the First World War* (Manchester).

Bewsher, F. W. 1921. *The History of the 51st (Highland) Division, 1914–18* (Edinburgh).

Bond, Brian 2002. *The Unquiet Western Front* (Cambridge).

Busch (ed.), Briton C. 2003. *Canada and the Great War. Western Front Association Papers* (Montreal).

Digby, Peter K. 1993. *Pyramids and Poppies. The 1st SA Infantry Brigade in Libya, France and Flanders* (Rivonia).

Dowson, Roger J. 2000. *Manchester Scottish. The Story of the Manchester Contingent of the 15th Battalion Royal Scots 1914–18 with a Record of Manchester and Salford Men who Served in the Regiment* (Manchester).

Ewing, John 1921. *The History of the 9th (Scottish) Division* (London).

Graves, Dianne 1997. *A Crown of Life: the World of John McCrae* (Staplehurst).

Grey, Jeffrey 1999. *A Military History of Australia* (Cambridge).

Harding, Brian 2001. *Keeping Faith. The History of the Royal British Legion* (Barnsley).

Harris, Stephen J. 1988. *Canadian Brass: the Making of a Professional Army, 1860–1939* (Toronto).

Haycock, Ronald 1986. *Sam Hughes: the Public Career of a Controversial Canadian, 1885–1916* (Waterloo).

Inglis, K. S. assisted by Jan Brazier 1998. *Sacred Places: War Memorials in the Australian Landscape* (Carlton).

McCartney, Helen B. 2005. *Citizen Soldiers. The Liverpool Territorials in the First World War* (Cambridge).

MacKenzie, David (ed.) 2005. *Canada and the First World War. Essays in Honour of Robert Craig Brown* (Toronto).

Mackenzie, John M. with Nigel R. Dalziel 2007. *The Scots in South Africa. Ethnicity, Identity, Gender and Race, 1772–1914* (Manchester).

Maclean, Chris and Jock Phillips 1990. *The Sorrow and the Pride: New Zealand War Memorials* (Wellington).

Macleod, Jenny (ed.) 2012 *Gallipoli. Making History* (London).

Murdoch, Steve and A. Mackillop (eds) 2002. *Fighting for Identity: Scottish Military Experience c.1550–1900* (Leiden).

Nasson, Bill 2007. *Springboks on the Somme. South Africa in the Great War 1914–1918* (Johannesburg).

Nicholson, Gerald W. L. 1962. *The Canadian Expeditionary Force, 1914–19* (Ottawa).

Orpen, Neil 1986. *The Cape Town Highlanders 1885–1985* (Cape Town).

Pugsley, Christopher 1998. *Gallipoli. The New Zealand Story* (Auckland).

Pugsley, Christopher 2004, *The ANZAC Experience. New Zealand, Australia and Empire in the First World War* (Auckland).

Sheffield, Gary 2001. *Forgotten Victory. The First World War: Myths and Realities* (London).

Speed, Brigadier F. W. 1988. *Esprit De Corps. The History of the Victorian Scottish Regiment and the 5th Infantry Battalion* (Sydney).

Spiers, Edward M., Jeremy A. Crang and Matthew J. Strickland 2012. *A Military History of Scotland* (Edinburgh).

Stephenson, Michael 2012. *The Last Full Measure. How Soldiers Die in Battle* (New York).

Stewart, Graham and John Sheen 1999. *Tyneside Scottish. 20th, 21st, 22nd & 23rd (Service) Battalions of the Northumberland Fusiliers. A History of the Tyneside Scottish Brigade Raised in the North East in World War One* (Barnsley).

Streets, Heather 2004. *Martial Races. The Military, Race and Masculinity in British Imperial Culture, 1857–1914* (Manchester).

Wineguard, Timothy C. 2012. *Indigenous Peoples of the British Dominions and the First World War* (Cambridge).

The Bagpipes of
James Richardson VC

16TH (CANADIAN SCOTTISH) BATTALION
CANADIAN EXPEDITIONARY FORCE

THE BAGPIPING HERITAGE OF THE SCOTTISH regiments the the British army was an integral part of the Scottish military tradition. The manner in which that tradition was carried forward on the battlefields of the First World War was a matter of pride, and comfort, for those in Scotland and with Scottish links, something familiar amidst the unprecedented scale of the Great War.[1] This set of bagpipes represents the migration of that tradition. The pipes date to the early years of the twentieth century. The bag is covered in the Lennox tartan and the drones are made from Blackwood, the traditional wood for this part of the instrument. The tuning slides on the drone and the round sole at the end of the chanter are made of ivory. The pipes are incomplete through damage, the result of their having lain unclaimed on a Great War battlefield for some months before their eventual recovery.

The story of James Richardson and his pipes is both poignant and pertinent to the broader narrative of the Scottish diaspora at war. It encapsulates the experience of a young, newly arrived Scottish emigrant to Canada who, soon after his arrival, volunteered to defend his recently left homeland and the British empire. Sadly, as with many others who had made similar journeys, he was to make the ultimate sacrifice.

Jimmy Richardson was born in Bellshill in the very heart of industrial Lanarkshire, the powerhouse of the Scottish economy which had given the west of Scotland the epithet 'the workshop of the world'. He was educated at Auchinwraith Public School in Blantyre, Bellshill Academy, and John Street School in Glasgow.[2] Immediately before leaving for Canada the Richardson family is believed to have been living in Rutherglen, a town to the south of Glasgow. According to his emigration records, Richardson was an electrician to trade. This was a typical occupation for one of the large throng of young Scotsman who entered Canada in the years before the Great War. A large proportion of this emigrant group were highly skilled tradesmen.

Richardson emigrated to Canada in 1913 on board the *Parisian*, the first large steamer of the famous Allan Line. Leaving from Glasgow, he travelled with his father, David, and two of his younger siblings, Alice and David. The Richardson party landed at Halifax, Nova Scotia, on 23 May 1913, this being one of Canada's major ports for the disembarkation of emigrants.[3] They then made the 6000 km overland journey by rail to reach British Columbia, their chosen destination for their new life in Canada. Very soon after his arrival in Vancouver, aged 17½, Richardson enrolled with the cadet corps of the 72nd Regiment, the Seaforth Highlanders of Canada.

The origins of this regiment date back to 1909, when members of a number of Vancouver's leading Scottish associational groups came together to discuss the proposal of raising a highland regiment for the city. After canvassing for potential backing for this initiative, a meeting to discuss the issue was held on 11 May 1909 in the rooms of St Andrews and Caledonian Societies, and the idea was received favourably by all of those present.

As support for the regiment was more widely canvassed, the united Scottish societies obtained authorisation from the Minister of Militia in Ottawa to raise the regiment and also the designation of the highly significant number '72', which was then vacant on the Canadian Militia list. This number was a link to a distinguished Scottish highland regiment: the Seaforth Highlanders. The much-desired official recognition of their affiliation with Seaforth Highlanders in the home country came on 15 April 1912 when the regiment received official consent to use the name 72nd Seaforth Highlanders of Canada. With it, they would wear the Seaforth regimental tartan and similar insignia.

The next logical step was for the Canadian Seaforths to form a Regimental Pipes and Drums. This they did, and it retains today the distinction of being the oldest continuously active pipe band in British Columbia. Two years after its initial formation the Canadian Seaforths established a cadet force. The desire to find like-minded friends in a strange city, and the prospect of continuing to play the pipes, must have encouraged Richardson to join the Seaforth cadets.[4]

While living with his family in Rutherglen, Richardson had been a keen Boy Scout. Given his speedy enlistment into the cadets and the regimental pipe band, it can be assumed that he was already an accomplished piper back home in Scotland. His skill is borne out by newspaper

Below:

The earliest extant photograph of Cadet James Richardson (extreme right) of the Seaforth Highlanders of Canada.

By the kind permission of the Commanding Officer of the Seaforth Highlanders of Canada reports which indicate that he was a regular competitor on the highland games circuit, appearing at Vancouver, North Vancouver, and on Vancouver Island in the gatherings held at the provincial capital, Victoria. Not only was Richardson a regular competitor, he was also consistently successful. At the time of Richardson's death, his father David had in his possession three gold medals for piping won by his late son.

Even before the advent of the war, Richardson had demonstrated great personal courage, in his response to an incident in 1914 during the course of an ordinary working day. As a skilled tradesman, he had found employment in a Vancouver factory situated close to an inlet of the Pacific Ocean known as False Creek, which at that time was at the heart of the city's industrial district. A call went up that a young boy had fallen into the water and was in danger of drowning. The young Richardson immediately ran outside to help, diving into the creek in what unfortunately turned out to be a vain attempt to save the youth's life. A similar display of personal bravery would then be played out two short years later at the Battle of the Somme in October 1916.

On the outbreak of the First Word War in August 1914, Richardson volunteered for service in the Canadian Expeditionary Force (CEF). He was 'taken on strength' on 23 September 1914 at Valcartier Base, Québec, enlisted as a private, and , given his musical prowess, as a piper with the 16th Infantry Battalion (The Canadian Scottish) CEF, for which the Seaforths provided the largest contingent consisting of 25 officers and 514 men. Initially the Canadian Seaforths had been refused the request of their Commanding Officer to be sent overseas as a separate unit.[5]

Although refused permission to serve overseas, the Canadian Seaforths were nevertheless highly effective recruiting agents around the city of Vancouver. Through their efforts a further 41 officers and 1637 other ranks were recruited for deployment to a number of the newly created CEF battalions destined for overseas service. Richardson joined an amalgamated pipe band made up of pipers and drummers from the three other Canadian Militia regiments integrated to form the 16th Battalion CEF: the 91st Canadian Highlanders (Argyll and Sutherland

Below:

15th Battalion (48th Highlanders of Canada), CEF, at Valcartier.

© 48th Highlanders Museum

Highlanders), the 79th Queen's Own Cameron Highlanders, and the 50th Regiment (Gordon Highlanders), a regiment of fellow British Columbians from Victoria.[6]

Richardson arrived in France on St Valentine's Day 1915. Serving as part of 1st Canadian Division, the 16th Battalion had already seen action on several occasions before the Somme offensive of 1916. One of the most difficult was the Battle of Ancre Heights on 8 October 1916, which had as its main objective the seizure of the heavily defended Regina Trench, the longest German trench on the Western Front. The 16th Battalion's part in the assault was centred just to the north of the nearby village of Courcelette.

The advancing Canadians crossed 'No Man's Land' in the face of enemy rifles, machine guns, mortars and artillery. The traditional role of the company piper was to play alongside his comrades, and to encourage them forward to battle. Although not originally detailed for the attack on Regina Trench that day, the 20-year-old Richardson pleaded successfully with his commanding officer to be allowed to accompany the troops, whom he piped over the top. The advancing company encountered a barrage of enemy fire and almost intractable wire which the preceding artillery barrage had failed to cut.[7]

At this desperate point, with the company commander killed and the casualties mounting, Richardson volunteered to pipe one more time. He reportedly called out to Company Sergeant-Major Arden Mackie, 'Wull I gie them wund [wind]?' Keen to see morale and momentum restored from its dangerously low ebb, Mackie replied without hesitation, 'Aye mon, gie 'em wind'.[8] For some ten minutes, fully exposed to the view of the enemy, Richardson 'strode up and down outside the wire, playing his pipes with the greatest coolness', while a 'storm of fire swirled past him on either side'. The citation to Richardson's gallantry decoration later elaborated on the situation: 'The effect was instantaneous. Inspired by his splendid example, the company rushed the wire with such fury and determination that the obstacle was overcome and the position captured.'[9]

The Battalion's commanding officer who made the Victoria Cross recommendation was Lieutenant-Colonel C. W. Peck VC. Though not a Scot, on the efficacy of the use of the pipes Peck was adamant that 'the purpose of war is to win victories, and if one can do this better by encouraging certain sentiments and traditions, why shouldn't it be done?'[10]

Given his opinion of the significance of pipers in the field, unsurprisingly it was Peck, who was then a major and Richardson's company commander, who made the recommendation at the time that Richardson should receive the VC for his conspicuous bravery on the day. However, for technical reasons there was a two-year delay before the award was finally gazetted on 22 October 1918.

Later in the attack, Richardson participated in bombing operations (grenade-throwing) during which he and his company sergeant-major captured two Germans in a dug-out. Shortly afterwards, Richardson was ordered to escort the now-wounded company sergeant-major and the two prisoners back to the British lines. As he led them away, he suddenly realised that during the recovery of his wounded comrade and the two prisoners he had left his pipes on the battlefield. Despite being told by his company commander to leave the pipes where they lay, Richardson placed his wounded comrade and the two prisoners in the relative safety of a nearby shell-hole.

Returning into 'No Man's Land', Richardson was thought to have been hit by enemy fire. He was initially listed as missing in action and, as he was never seen again, was officially presumed to have died on 8 or 9 October 1916.

On 22 October 1918 Richardson was posthumously awarded the Victoria Cross, the highest British award for gallantry, for his actions at Regina Trench. He was one of four members of the 16th Battalion to win this ultimate award, one of whom was another Lanarkshire lad, Private William Johnstone Milne from Cambusnethan.

However, it is the fate and rediscovery of Richardson's pipes themselves that make for an intriguing detective story. Up until 2006 the pipes were displayed at Ardvrek School, a preparatory school near Crieff in Perthshire. It would appear that the pipes were brought to the school a few years after the Great War by the Revd Major Edward Yeld Bate. Mr Tomas Christie, father of a pupil at the school, became interested in the pipes and began to research their origins. According to a card which had been kept with the pipes during their time at Ardvreck School, these were the 'bagpipes found on the battlefield of the Somme near Courcelette in February 1917'.[11]

One theory is that Bate, as an army chaplain, might have presided at Richardson's initial burial. Research suggests that Bate, in his involvement with the repatriation of the dead from the field of battle, may have either come across the pipes himself or was presented with them. Unfortunately Bate did not commit to paper an explanation of his role in the discovery of the pipes; given the provenance on this card, it is difficult to come to any conclusion other than it was through Bate's role in post-battle repatriations that the pipes eventually ended up at Ardvrek School. Presumably due to Bate's continuing, and under-standable, assumption that the pipes were Scottish, he presented them to Ardvrek at his departure from the school in the early 1930s, before taking up a teaching position in England.

Thus there is a sound reason to believe the pipes were in Bate's possession in the years before his appointment to the school. The other key piece of material evidence linking the pipes to Richardson was the fact that the pipe was covered in the Lennox tartan; this tartan had not been adopted by any Scottish regiment. Further investigation into the units which served in the vicinity of Courcelette revealed that no Scottish regiment fought on that length of the Western Front.

From the earliest years of their formation, the Canadian Seaforths adopted the Seaforth MacKenzie tartan of their associated Imperial regiment. However, the military authorities were of the firm opinion that members of the new battalion must relinquish all attachments to their former militia regiments, and forge a new loyalty to their Expeditionary Force battalion. The first regimental historian of the 16th Battalion described this situation in terms that a 'new clan or family had to begin'. This new fighting clan had to make its own mark and invent its own traditions around which it could fight as a cohesive unit.

On 16 December 1914, while training on Salisbury Plain, the battalion was granted its unifying subtitle which summed up its common cause: 'The Canadian Scottish'.

Even while en route to England the 16th Battalion was still dressed in the four different uniforms, tartans and cap badges of its constituent companies. Richardson's pipe bag was covered in the Lennox tartan which was a distinctive choice. It was this tartan which first heightened interest in this set of pipes and led the investigation of the fact that these pipes might be those of Richardson.

The reason for choosing the Lennox tartan was prosaic, but not entirely unusual. The wife of the battalion's founding commanding officer, Lieutenant-Colonel J. E. Leckie, was of the Lennox family. Thus the pipers and drummers of the 16th Battalion were kitted out in the Lennox tartan as a compliment to her. Leckie was well attuned to the martial traditions of the Highland regiments and keen that his pipers should continue the tradition of playing the battalion into battle. It was important that they should have a regimental tartan of their own.

Retired Pipe Major Roger McGuire of the Canadian Scottish Regiment has recently conducted research into Richardson's initial burial and the subsequent exhumation which established that he had been removed from plot 57C.M.16.A.4.6 on 15 June 1920.[12] Richardson's remains had been identified from the cross placed on the grave by the Graves Registration Unit at the time of the original burial. Unfortunately the Commonwealth War Graves Commission did not have any record of who was actually present at his initial burial. Richardson's remains, and those of his fallen comrades, were then re-interred at Adanac Cemetery, Miraumont, close to Courcelette, a cemetery made from the graves brought in from the surrounding battlefields. The name 'Adanac' is simply Canada spelled backwards.

One rather curious press report in the *Manitoba Free Press* on 5 December 1918, not long after Richardson's family accepted his Victoria Cross, categorically states that Richardson's body was found on the morning of 10 October 1916. This article was based on the testimony of an officer of another Canadian battalion which had been detailed to take over the sector of the line previously held by the 16th Battalion. While bringing back the men who had been wounded during the attacks of the previous day when Richardson had piped, the unnamed officer stated that 'an officer from an adjoining company came upon the body of a piper and the blood-stained pipes'.

Below:

Richardson's family at his gravestone at Adanac Cemetery.

© David Boulding

Another complicating factor was the death of a second piper on the same day. This casualty was Piper John Parks who had been a member of the pipe band of the pre-war 50th Regiment (Gordon Highlanders) of Victoria, before being assigned to the 16th Battalion CEF along with his comrades. Could the pipes, now said to be those belonging to Richardson, have actually belonged to Parks? Piping experts, including Roger McGuire, closely examined surviving photographs of the 16th Battalion's pipe band. Looking at the pipes carried by Richardson and Parks respectively, he noted among the distinguishing features that the soles of each of the two chanters were quite different. On this comparison, the pipes could be identified with confidence to be those of James Richardson.

By this attribution, the pipes became a significant artefact in the history of British Columbia, and in the story of Canada and the First World War. At the time of his enlistment, Richardson recorded his father, David Richardson, as the chief of police in the town of Chilliwack, BC. Thus in 2003, in the grounds of the Museum at Chilliwack, Richardson was commemorated by a life-size bronze statue of him playing the pipes. Finally, in a public ceremony on 8 November 2006, the bagpipes themselves were formally returned from Scotland to the British Columbia Legislature in Victoria. This place of honour, in the main foyer of the Legislative Assembly building, is now their permanent home.

Below:

Richardson's repatriated pipes carried by Cadet Josh MacDonald of the Canadian Scottish Regiment (Princess Mary's).

Times columnist, Victoria, British Columbia

Pipe banner

of the 92nd Battalion
Canadian Expeditionary Force, *c.*1916

A pipe banner is designed to be tied to the bass drone, the largest of the pipes in a set of bagpipes. As a feature of the material culture of military bagpiping, the banners are an inheritance from older highland traditions. The personal pipers who once formed part of the retinue of a clan chief or lesser highland dignitary might display the armorial banner of their chief hung from the pipes. Within Scottish regiments of the British army, officers commanding companies and those ranks above would enjoy the privilege of providing a personal banner for one piper. Even in a hastily organised Canadian Expeditionary Force battalion, each company might have a banner for its piper. In this instance, the banner has been emblazoned with the regiment's title and decorated with two kilted highland soldiers and the regimental badge in the style of a clan-style crest, with the Gaelic motto *Dileas Gu Brath* (Faithful Forever). These designs have been sewn onto a panel, which in turn has been sewn onto a larger piece of khaki material. These basic materials and the rather crude construction are in marked contrast to the silk and heavily embroidered banners more usually carried by military pipers. This is an artefact which speaks of the haste and improvisation whereby Canadian Expeditionary Force battalions were recruited, organised and equipped.

That such trouble should have been taken to create artefacts such as this speaks volumes about the need felt among a number of the CEF battalions to take on a specifically Scottish regimental identity and to reflect Scottish martial traditions. Since the existing 'Scottish' Canadian

militia units were barred from going to war under their designation, some of the new battalions sought to perpetuate a conspicuous and self-conscious highland image, with kilts and pipe bands.

This mix of identities was often complex; many Canadian Scots fought in CEF battalions devoid of any obvious Scottish connection. The flip-side to this was of course that many soldiers who had no connection to Scotland volunteered or found themselves recruited into some of Canada's most visibly Scottish battalions.

The badge and motto were derived from the cap badge of a pre-First World War militia regiment based in Toronto, the 48th Highlanders of Canada. It was from the nucleus of this unit that most of the raw recruits for the 92nd Battalion CEF were drawn. The 92nd was one of three overseas battalions which were raised with recruits from around the city of Toronto by the 48th Highlanders of Canada for service during the war. The 48th also successfully recruited a number of extra companies equal in size to two further battalions for other units of the CEF.[13]

The battalion was authorised on 30 July 1915 as the 92nd Overseas Battalion, CEF and embarked for Britain on 20 May 1916. However, the battalion never went to war as a single unit. By the time the men of the 92nd were in training in England, their main function was to provide reinforcements for other units of the Canadian Corps in the field. Finally on 24 January 1917, the 92nd's remaining body of men was absorbed by the 5th Reserve Battalion, CEF. Eventually the inevitable took place and the 92nd ceased to exist as a separate unit when it was disbanded on 1 September 1917.

Clearly, the lure of such Scottish iconography was a powerful tool, consciously employed by the battalions and their recruiting agents. Such imagery was used on recruitment posters designed to strike a chord with prospective volunteers, in an attempt to appeal to their most emotive attachments to their homeland and their Scottish identity. Such recruitment propaganda was just as much aimed at emigrants of Scottish ancestry who had been born in Canada, as it was intended to target the many newly arrived young Scotsmen, such as James Richardson in Vancouver.

Below:

Recruitment poster for the 236th New Brunswick Kilties Battalion, CEF.

© Imperial War Museum
PST 12467

Guy Drummond

A Personal Story

Guy Drummond was born on 15 August 1887 to Sir George Alexander Drummond and his second wife Grace Julia Parker, and so into a wealthy and influential family who were at the very top of Montreal society. To use the parlance of the city, they were one of the 'Square Mile' anglophone families, those who tended to live in the up-market area at the foot of Mount Royal itself, the hill which gave its name to the city.

Drummond's father was a successful industrialist and financier, and a senator in the Canadian upper house. Drummond was naturally drawn to a career in public service. After studying for a degree at McGill University, he travelled to Europe to pursue further studies in social sciences at the *École libre des sciences politiques* in Paris, a highly prestigious place of advanced study for the political and diplomatic elites of French society.

Drummond was attracted to the world of politics, just like his father, and he became actively involved with the Conservative Party in Montreal. As one facet of his desire to be engaged in public service, Drummond enlisted as a junior officer in the 5th Regiment, Royal Highlanders of Canada. This militia unit, founded in 1862, had taken on its Scottish name in October 1906, and was Montreal's only 'highland' regiment.[14] Clearly the martial tradition of the Royal Highlanders of Canada appealed to Drummond's sense of his Scottish roots. His father, Sir George, had been born in Edinburgh in 1829.

At the time of Drummond's enlistment, the Royal Highlanders were commanded by Lieutenant-Colonel George S. Cantlie, another leading light of the higher echelons of Montreal Scottish society. Drummond was commissioned as a lieutenant in 'H' Company of the regiment's 1st Battalion early in 1912, and appointed company commander the following year with the rank of captain.

In April 1914, Drummond married Mary

Hendrie Braithwaite and the young couple left Canada for a honeymoon in Europe. They were still in Europe when Britain declared war on Germany on 4 August 1914. The newly-weds returned home and, true to his commitment to the service of his country, Drummond volunteered for war service in the European continent he had just left behind. In September 1914 he joined 13th Battalion (Royal Highlanders of Canada) CEF, a battalion which had been raised around a core of volunteers from the militia unit of the same name. The 13th Battalion sailed with the first Canadian contingent to be sent to England and eventually formed part of the Canadian 3rd Brigade, along with a number of other CEF battalions with overt Scottish identities. As for many militia officers seeking places in the Expeditionary Force, Drummond had to relinquish his senior rank and travelled overseas with his new battalion as a lieutenant.

Drummond and his battalion landed in France in February 1915, and on 21 April they were detailed to relieve another Montreal unit at the front line close to St Julien, a village a few kilometres north of Ypres in Belgium. Only the following day, the 13th Battalion was caught up in major German artillery bombardment, followed by the first chlorine gas attack in history. Drummond was with the support company which was required to engage directly with German troops who had taken the opportunity to attack an opening in the front line. Drummond attempted to encourage the men who fled from the gas clouds in their panic.[15] His ability to speak fluent French[16] was critical here, and many of the fleeing allied troops finally rallied to hold the line.[17]

Sadly, Drummond was one of the earliest casualties in this battle – shot through the throat. He became one of twelve officers (including the commanding officer) and 454 from other ranks who were lost in the engagement which came to be known as the Second Battle of Ypres. These losses represented a half of the fighting force of the 13th Battalion.

Poignantly, Drummond's wife Mary gave birth to a son on 1 October 1915

Below:

Guy Drummond (with hand in pocket) at the Western Front, 1915.

McCord Museum, Montreal
M2004.160.135

63

who, as with many children of the Great War, would never know his father. To compound this loss for the family, one of Drummond's sisters-in-law was drowned on 7 May 1915 on board the *Lusitania* when the liner was struck by a torpedo from a German U-boat. She had been on her way to England to comfort Drummond's distraught young widow. Drummond's son, also named Guy, served as a pilot with the Royal Canadian Air Force during the Second World War.[18]

After the War, Drummond's family commissioned a half-life-size statue of Guy, to commemorate their much-loved son. This was sculpted by Robert Tait McKenzie, another Canadian with Scottish roots. For many years the statue was displayed in the Canadian Senate Library, before it was transferred to the Canadian War Museum, Ottawa, where it is now forms part of the Beaverbrook Collection of War Art.[19]

Above:

Statue of Drummond.

Robert McKenzie, Captain Guy Drummond, CWM 19780063-001, Beaverbrook Collection of War Art, © Canadian War Museum

Notes

1 The wartime achievements of pipers, including the piper featured here, were soon collated and commemorated in the classic work by Seton and Grant 1920.

2 *Canadian Dictionary of Biography* entry on James Cleland Richardson VC: http://www.biographi.ca/en/bio/richardson_james_cleland_14E.html

3 The authors are grateful to Mrs Carole Wilson of Glenlyon for sharing genealogical research on Richardson's family.

4 The authors are grateful to Paul Ferguson, Curator of the Chilliwack Museum, for supplying information on Richardson's early years in Vancouver. See also Creagh and Humphris (eds) n.d., pp. 297–8.

5 Wendy Ugolini, 'Scottish Commonwealth Regiments', in Spiers, Crang and Strickland 2012, p. 496.

6 D. M. Drysdale n.d., p. 1.

7 The fullest account of the battle is in the battalion's official history: Urquhart 1932, pp. 180–7.

8 Zeuhlke 2008.

9 *London Gazette* 30967, 22 October 1918.

10 Drysdale n.d., p. 2.

11 A copy of the original card survives in the archives of the Legislative Assembly of British Columbia.

12 The author is grateful to Roger McGuire for generously sharing his research on James Richardson.

13 The Government of Canada has some excellent web-based resources for Canadian military history. Much of the detailed information on the origins and antecedents of the various regiments in this chapter has been drawn from the Official Lineages pages: http://www.cmp-cpm.forces.gc.ca/dhh-dhp/his/ol-lo/index-eng.asp

14 http://www.cmp-cpm.forces.gc.ca/dhh-dhp/his/ol-lo/vol-tom-3/par2/bwc-eng.asp

15 For a more detailed account of the battle, see Hutchison 1962, pp. 74–5 and Fetherstonhaugh 1925, pp. 44–5.

16 The author is grateful to Earl John Chapman, for sharing his short biographical sketch of Guy Drummond, originally published in *Canada's Red Hackle*, the Journal of the Black Watch (Royal Highland Regiment) of Canada, issue no.12, Autumn 2008, pp. 14–15.

17 Fetherstonhaugh 1925, p. 45.

18 Earl John Chapman, short biographical sketch of Guy Drummond, in *Canada's Red Hackle* 12, Autumn 2008, 12, p. 15.

19 Canadian War Museum, acc. no. 19780063-001.

Bibliography

Creagh, Sir O'Moore and E. M. Humphris (eds) n.d. *The Victoria Cross, 1856–1920* (Polstead, Suffolk).

Drysdale, D. M. n.d. 'Pipe Band of the 16th Battalion (Canadian Scottish) CEF', unpublished paper.

Fetherstonhaugh, R. C. 1925. *The 13th Battalion Royal Highlanders of Canada, 1914–1919* (Montreal).

Hutchison, Paul P. 1962. *Canada's Black Watch: The First Hundred Years, 1862–1962* (Montreal).

Seton, Sir Bruce and Piper-Major John Grant 1920. *The Pipes of War. A Record of the Achievements of Pipers of Scottish and Overseas Regiments during the War 1914–18* (Glasgow).

Spiers, Edward M., Jeremy Crang and Matthew Strickland 2012. *A Military History of Scotland*.

Urquhart, H. M. 1932. *The History of the 16th Battalion (the Canadian Scottish) Canadian Expeditionary Force in the Great War, 1914–1919* (Toronto).

Zeuhlke, Mark 2008. *Brave Battalion: the remarkable saga of the 16th Battalion (Canadian Scottish) in the First World War* (Mississauga).

Featured objects

Bagpipes of James Richardson VC of the 16th (Canadian Scottish) Battalion, Canadian Expeditionary Force on loan from the British Columbia Legislative Assembly. National Museums Scotland loan no. IL.2013.21.

Pipe banner of the 92nd Battalion, CEF, *c.*1916 (National Museums Scotland acc. no. M.2007.26).

Australians

Defence of Anzac

BRONZE SCULPTURE
BY WALLACE ANDERSON, 1933

Opening page, left:

Lieutenant W. W. Anderson (front centre), with staff of the Australian Modelling Section, Lille, France, 1919.

Australian War Memorial EO5912

Opening page, right:

Defence of ANZAC, bronze sculpture by Wallace Anderson, 1933.

Australian War Memorial ART 13664

Below:

Australians at Quinn's Post, ANZAC line, Gallipoli, 29 May, 1915.

© Imperial War Museum HU 50622

THERE IS NOTHING OSTENSIBLY SCOTTISH ABOUT Wallace Anderson's bronze sculpture depicting two Australian soldiers during the Gallipoli campaign of 1915. This is a quintessentially Australian work of art. The two figures represent the idealised characteristics which the Australian population, and the wider world, had come to recognise and expect from the soldiers of Australia in the aftermath of the Great War. First of all, the figures are both wearing the slouch hats with which Australians were identified, brims down as protection against the sun of Turkey's Gallipoli peninsula. And, with an informality which might be found surprising in soldiers of virtually any other nationality, they are wearing relatively little else. Both are in shorts, boots and socks. One wears a short-sleeved shirt; the other is bare-chested. They are healthy physical specimens, redolent of youth and strength. They appear determined but relaxed, more civilian than military in bearing.

This is a classic image of the Australians at Gallipoli, the campaign which defined Australian public memory of the First World War. These two Australian soldiers are defending the beachhead perimeter known itself as 'ANZAC' after the Australian and New Zealand Army Corps forces which captured it by amphibious assault on 25 April 1915, and from which they failed to break-out thereafter through the high-ground commanded by their Ottoman Turkish opponents. The figures appear unbowed by their exposure to debilitating conditions, to disease, and to the dogged resistance of their enemies in the Gallipoli trenches.

Their irregular appearance conforms to the image which was first transmitted to the public by the English war correspondent Ellis Ashmead-Bartlett in his reports of the landings, and later celebrated in his documentary film of the campaign.[1] In his admiration for the size and physique of the Anzac soldiers, Ashmead-Bartlett impressed the newspaper-reading and cinema-going public in Britain and Australia with his reports of a 'race of athletes', and of a 'naked army' performing prodigious feats of military endurance in the Aegean sun.[2] The influential Australian war correspondent Charles Bean represented his fellow countrymen in similar glowing terms, comparing their appearance favourably with the less imposing figures of the youth of Britain serving in the same campaign.[3] Gallipoli was only the beginning for Australian participation in the First World War, but this was the image which stuck. Anderson's figures are archetypes now known as 'Diggers'. This colloquial appellation was given first to New Zealand troops on the Somme in 1916, but was later appropriated by the Australians. The Digger signifies a national self-image of informality and initiative, of independence of spirit with a casual disregard for military discipline and, above all, of outstanding courage and soldierly ability.[4]

Above:

Wallace Anderson, 1938

Courtesy of the Anderson family

The Scottish connection lies with the artist. The sculptor Wallace Anderson (1888–1975) was an Australian born and bred, as were his parents. But Anderson's paternal grandfather and both of his maternal grandparents had emigrated from Scotland in the middle decades of the nineteenth century, the former from Ayrshire and the latter from Edinburgh and Dundee respectively. The Scottish influence ran strong in the family. Anderson referred light-heartedly in his unpublished memoirs to 'clan Anderson'.[5] While Anderson was growing up in Dean, Victoria (later moving to Ballarat and Geelong), his father William was an elder in the Presbyterian 'Scotch Church'. Anderson senior was a figure of some influence, serving for a time as a Member of the Legislative Assembly of Victoria. A clue to the strength of his feelings about the old country may be discerned in the name he gave to his son, because Wallace Anderson shared, although did not habitually use, the Christian name of his father, making him in full William Wallace Anderson, a homage to William Wallace, Guardian of Scotland, one of the two Scottish heroes of the 13th and 14th century Wars of Independence.[6] Anderson's memories of his migrant grandfather Charles Naples were of a man 'very proud of his Scottish ancestry', although half-Italian, a member of the local highland society and given to kilt-wearing, who hung his dining room with prints of Landseer's highland sporting landscapes.[7]

When war broke out in 1914, Anderson had progressed from studying engineering and taking art classes in the evenings to a position as an art teacher in the Technical School at Sunshine, a suburb of Melbourne. By his own account, 'being such a dreamer I never thought of the war', but his brother thought otherwise and had obtained an officer's commission in a Light Horse unit, in which capacity he had served at Gallipoli.[8] It was his brother's return home, wounded and suffering from the effects of dysentery, one of the scourges of that campaign, which prompted Wallace Anderson to enlist. Joining the 23rd Battalion of the Australian Imperial Force, he capitalised on his earlier experience as a senior sergeant in a school cadet corps and quickly advanced through the ranks, earning the distinction of obtaining an officer's commission as a 2nd Lieutenant even before his battalion embarked for active service in Europe. A few weeks before embarkation, in May 1916, he married Gladys Andrews in the Presbyterian Scots Church, Melbourne.

Anderson's journey to the Western Front was a long one, in the troopship HMAT *Armadale* to Southampton, via Durban and Cape Town, to a camp on Salisbury Plain. Selected to train as an instructor at a bombing school in France, where he taught the proper throwing of grenades, he was separated from his battalion, and when he finally joined it and moved up to front-line trenches opposite the high ground of the Butte de Warlencourt, he had been promoted to Lieutenant. With 'C' Company of the 23rd Battalion, in 6th Brigade of the Australian 2nd Division, he served in actions in the Albert sector, at Moquet Farm and at Bullecourt. In his time at the Front he contracted pleurisy, was hit but fortunately unharmed by a spent bullet, and survived through an unsuccessful Brigade attack on enemy positions, prior to which he had surveyed his battalion's objectives by nightfall in No Man's Land with a small reconnaissance party. His luck ran out shortly afterwards when, withdrawn to a rest area miles from the front, he was wounded by the fall of a 'whizzbang' shell. Shortly after returning to his unit, he received the double blow of news that his brother had been killed in action in Palestine, and that his wife was recovering from the loss of their stillborn child. At this low point, an earlier acquaintance with a fellow officer from training in England brought him into the orbit of Captain C. E. W. Bean, war correspondent and author of *The ANZAC Book*, who had already done much to promote the legend of Australian and New Zealand troops at Gallipoli, as would be epitomised by Anderson's later sculpture.[9]

Anderson was invited by Bean to serve with the Australian War

Records Section, a unit dedicated to collecting and compiling unit war diaries, the reports of action kept for the purpose of writing the *Official History of Australia in the War*, the chronicle whereby Bean as editor was to consolidate his vision of the natural prowess of the Australian soldier.[10] Bean was already lobbying for the second strand of his commemorative plans, a great Australian national museum of the war, where collections of artefacts, photographs, film, letters and diaries would be amassed in order to ensure that the sacrifice of Australians would not be forgotten and that later generations would understand the significance of Australia's arrival on the international stage. Anderson began work as Museums Officer by collecting artefacts for the putative museum, touring front line units in the early months of 1918 returning to store depots in a vehicle loaded 'with all sorts of relics and souvenirs', and moving back and forth between London and the front on this business.[11]

It was after the armistice that Anderson's abilities as a sculptor came to the fore in his contributions to the collections of what ultimately became the Australian War Memorial in Canberra. Based in London with two fellow sculptors, he went on extensive tours of the battlefields of the recent conflict to research a series of dioramas and plan models depicting outstanding Australian feats of arms, as at Lone Pine, Gallipoli, and at the battle of Romani in the Sinai. Over a number of years, working in London and on his return to Australia, Anderson led and collaborated on the production of these innovative, painstakingly accurate models, which would later become key exhibits in the galleries of the Memorial.[12] Also prominent in the early displays were the bronze sculptures which Anderson and others produced independently on commission from the Memorial. *Defence of Anzac* is one of these, alongside his earlier *Water Carrier*, and *Evacuation*, each of which similarly mythologised the heroic 'Digger' in the Gallipoli setting. Anderson's sculpture also made an impact at a larger scale, with his bronze war memorials in public spaces in Geelong and other towns of Victoria, and, especially, with his 1935 statue of John Simpson and his donkey at the Shrine of Remembrance in Melbourne.[13] In this work he depicted a true story which had become a tenet of faith for the Anzac legend, that of a stretcher-bearer who nonchalantly braved enemy fire to evacuate the Gallipoli wounded down from the front line by donkey, until meeting his own death.

Writing his memoirs in the final years of his life, Anderson conformed to that view of the war which chimed with Australian nationalism, and which embraced his contemporary doubts about Australia's involvement in the war in Vietnam during the late 1960s and early 1970s. On reflection, he considered wars to be 'absolutely futile', a cynical product of the arms industry, and he described his dioramas for the Australian War Memorial as studies in 'the hideousness of war' rather than the works of patriotic hagiography they were intended to be at the point of commission, and as which they operated in Charles Bean's memorial vision.

The elder Anderson looked back with wonder at his youthful motivations for his voluntary enlistment to serve in the war, and repeated the view, widely held at that time, and still prevalent in Australia today, that the war was 'badly contrived and badly administered especially by the British senior officers under which at that time we were forced to obey'.[14] The bombast associated with the popular image of the Australian soldier is entirely absent from Anderson's modest and matter-of-fact memoirs, but he cannot fail to have been aware of the role which his sculpture and his modelling had played in setting the image of Australia as a new nation, one made in the crucible of a world war. His Scottish background played little part in this, which is why Anderson serves here as marker for how loyalties to home for a third-generation immigrant might mean identification above all with the land of their birth. His parents and grandparents might have instilled in him a strong sense of his Scottish ancestry and cultural inheritance, but in his war experiences, and in *Defence of Anzac* and his other war sculptures, William Wallace Anderson was an Australian through and through.

Slouch hat

from the uniform of
Major-General E. G. Sinclair-MacLagan,
Commanding 4th Division, Australian Imperial Force, 1918

By the end of the First World War the khaki felt slouch hat, with its broad brim usually turned up and buttoned to the crown on one side, had become an internationally recognised marker of Australian military identity and so a symbol of Australian nationhood itself. Volunteer mounted riflemen in the Australian colonies had begun wearing hats of this style in the 1880s, with local variations, and it was worn by many of the Australian volunteers who served in the South African War of 1899–1902.[15] Australia had no exclusive original claim on this item of military fashion; other mounted troops in South Africa had sported similar hats. They were hard-wearing, offered light and practical protection from sun and rain, rather than from the enemy, and with their leather chin straps were suitable riding apparel. For the same reasons, the slouch hat was appropriate military wear for the Australian climate. Just as importantly, it was evocative of an ideal of Australian manhood, associated with the hardy and resourceful life of the 'bushman' living at the frontier of an untamed interior, and when the new Commonwealth of Australia established its single army in 1903, the slouch hat was formally instituted as part of the army uniform for most of the troops.

The slouch hat was variously worn by military units with embellishments of insignia, coloured hat bands and the plumes of Australian birds, including the emu. But this particular example, with its plain khaki band, carries only a marker of national standardisation, the General Service cap badge known as 'the rising sun' first introduced for Australian volunteers on service in the South African War. While the rayed star design is indeed suggestive of a sun rising above the horizon, and so perhaps evocative of the geographic position and climate of the Australian continent, its origins are reputed instead to lie in the idea of representing a 'trophy of arms' composed of a semicircle of bayonet or sword blades.[16] Either way, these are arranged above the title in scroll 'Australian Commonwealth Military Forces' and around the central device of the British Imperial State Crown. The

Above:

Slouch hat from the uniform of Major-General E.G. Sinclair-MacLagan, Commanding 4th Division Australian Imperial Force, 1918.

National Museums Scotland

73

badge is therefore a marker of Australian difference, and national unity, but with the Crown keeping the symbolism firmly within the purview of the British empire.

Hat and badge together may therefore be recognised to have had decidedly British and colonial origins, but as a consequence of the Australian experience of the First World War they became indelibly associated with the Anzac ideal of independent national spirit. From 1916 onwards, Australian soldiers serving on the Western Front were issued with steel helmets, making their appearance more consistent with that of their British counterparts. But the slouch hat was the headgear associated with legendary performance of the Australian 'Digger' at Gallipoli, and with the successes more redolent of spirit of the bush won by mounted troops in Palestine and the Sinai. In post-war popular parlance, the slouch hat became the 'Digger Hat' and remains today, with a similar badge, part of the dress uniform of the Australian Army.

This particular hat was worn in the last years of the Great War, not by an Australian but by a Scotsman. It is marked inside with the name E. G. Sinclair-MacLagan, and the date 1918. At the end of the war, Major-General Ewen George Sinclair-MacLagan was a prominent Australian senior officer, commanding 4th Division of the Australian Imperial Force. As a non-Australian, he was unusual in this respect. In the early years of the war, Australian troops in the field were commanded at brigade level and upwards by British regular army staff officers. From May 1918 this changed as the Australian forces were 'nationalised' by grouping their divisions into a single corps, with Australian divisional commanders and with an Australian in overall charge in the figure of corps commander General Sir John Monash.

Sinclair-MacLagan was the only non-Australian to maintain his divisional command through this change. Born in Edinburgh in 1868, he was a career British soldier before the war, serving with the Border Regiment and the Yorkshire Regiment, including campaign service in India and in South Africa, where he was wounded and awarded the Distinguished Service Order. His connection with Australia commenced only in 1901, when he was posted for a period of three years to a staff officer role in military administration in New South Wales, combined with a position as adjutant of one of those Citizen Force part-time volunteer units which exhibited Scottish identity, the New South Wales Scottish Rifles.[17]

Sinclair-MacLagan accepted a second Australian posting in 1910, offered by a fellow Scot and senior Australian officer Brigadier-General William Bridges who would go on to become the first commander of the wartime Australian Imperial Force. It was as an officer on the staff of the new Australian Royal Military College at Duntroon that he became available for service with the Australian Imperial Force on the outbreak of war.

Appointed by Bridges to be commander of 3rd Australian Infantry Brigade in the Gallipoli campaign, Sinclair-MacLagan was in the thick of events that would fuel the Anzac legend, leading his brigade in the landings of 25 April 1915. It has been suggested that Sinclair-MacLagan might, on that first day, have inadvertently missed an opportunity to reach lightly defended high ground to the south, on account of his awareness that the Anzac forces had been landed further to the north than originally planned and his consequent decision to move troops south over concerns about the weakness of the right flank.[18] But his military abilities were never in question, and his steady head and professional acumen were instrumental in preventing the initial landing from turning into a disaster.

For his capable leadership, first of an Australian brigade and later of an Australian division on the Western Front, he was marked out as one British senior officer fully accepted and admired by the Australians under his command. In particular, his co-ordination of 4th Division's highly effective attack at Hamel in July 1918, executed in concert with American forces, was an outstanding demonstration of the military proficiency and confidence of Australian forces in the later years of the war.[19] In the view of one Australian historian, noting Sinclair-MacLagan's continuance in 1918 as the one British divisional commander in the Australian Corps, his pre-war pedigree with the Australian Military Forces meant 'he doubtless counted as an Australian'.[20] It was in this capacity, becoming in wartime an honorary Australian, fully committed to the military identity into which he had been absorbed, that Sinclair-MacLagan wore the symbolic slouch hat.

It is an open question whether Sinclair-MacLagan's Scottish background counted for anything with regard to the confidence placed in him by his adopted compatriots. There is some anecdotal evidence that in their habitual disregard for the abilities of British troops in comparison to their own, Australian soldiers were inclined to make an exception for the Scots, whose aggression, initiative and stamina were admired.[21] War correspondent Charles Bean was one who expressed views of this sort. When Bean repeated the suggestion, echoed in German propaganda, that Dominion troops were bearing a disproportionately

Above:

Colonel E. G. Sinclair MacLagan commanding 3rd Australian Infantry Brigade, Gallipoli, 1915.

© National Museums Scotland

high burden of the front-line fighting in 1918, because of their ability, experience and aggressive attitude, he allowed that all Scottish divisions, as well as a few of the other British divisions, were also being used as 'shock troops'.[22]

It seems more likely however that the trust placed in Sinclair-Mac-Lagan rested on his individual experience and competence rather than on any extension of admiration for the Scottish military tradition. He might best be described as an imperial soldier. As a Scotsman in the British army serving with English regiments, his short pre-war spell on secondment with the New South Wales Scottish Rifles had been his first encounter with the outward manifestations of Scottish military identity. That was until, continuing his professional military career after the end of the Great War, Sinclair-MacLagan received an appointment that reflected the distinction with which he had served Australia and the British empire. From 1919–23 he commanded 51st (Highland) Division, a wartime Scottish Territorial Force formation whose battlefield performance on the Western Front, when at its best, had accrued a place of honour in the eyes of the Scottish public. For this at least, he put aside his Australian slouch hat. But the hat he preserved for long afterwards, and passed it down through his family as a treasured memento of his Australian command.

Below:

Slouch hat-wearing pipers and drummers of the Australian 4th Machine Gun Company, Le Catalet, September, 1918.

Australian War Memorial E03269

William McDonald
A Personal Story

Among the collections of the Australian War Memorial in Canberra is a group of personal artefacts relating to the pre-war and Great War military service of William McDonald, of Stawell, Victoria, and latterly of Forest Lodge, New South Wales, who was Australian-born of Scottish descent. These objects include the uniform and insignia from his part-time service, ultimately as a warrant officer, with the New South Wales Scottish Rifles, a volunteer regiment which in 1911 became the 25th Infantry Battalion of Australia's Citizen Force. This was part-time soldiering, conducted while McDonald pursued a career as an employee of an electrical firm.[23] His scarlet wool highland doublet, for wearing with the regiment's 'Black Watch' tartan kilt, his plaid brooch and cap badge with Lion Rampant Scottish heraldic device, the portrait photographs of him in the full highland dress military uniform of which these are a part, are all a testament to the appeal of the Scottish tradition for men of McDonald's ancestry and martial propensities.

Below:

Staff Sergeant McDonald, New South Wales Scottish Rifles, c.1903.

Australian War Memorial PO3491.004

These are not, however, the garments and accoutrements in which McDonald went to war. As an under-age volunteer for the Australian contingent in the South African War of 1899–1902, he donned the khaki uniform and the slouch hat common to many of the imperial troops in that conflict, to serve as a corporal in the 1st New South Wales Mounted Infantry, receiving a mention in despatches for gallantry. McDonald volunteered again for active service on the outbreak of war in 1914, and it was in a similar uniform that he served as a Lieutenant in the 4th Battalion of the Australian Imperial Force. A 1914 studio portrait photograph, taken shortly before McDonald's departure in the troopship which took him towards Gallipoli, shows him as Honorary Lieutenant Quartermaster (his commission was confirmed on his arrival at Gallipoli) wearing Australian slouch hat and service dress uniform jacket adorned

with unit and Australian insignia, as well as the ribbon of his campaign service medal from South Africa.

At Gallipoli, McDonald was wounded twice, the second occasion during the celebrated Australian action at Lone Pine in August 1915 which, at dreadful cost, diverted enemy attention away from the New Zealand attack at Chunuk Bair to the north. For his courageous part in the Lone Pine battle, he was mentioned in despatches for a second time. Most remarkable among the collection relating to his service are a shrapnel ball and a 7.65 mm spent rifle bullet, both removed from the wounds he sustained, with a note in his own hand: 'Shrapnel Bullet that [I] was hit with first time. Rifle Bullet that hit me in the shoulder second time.' These mementoes of mortality he must have sent home to his wife and family as he recovered from his wounds. Promoted to Captain in March 1916, and serving again with 4th Battalion on the Western Front from early April, McDonald was killed in action on 16 August 1916 at Mouquet Farm, site of a sequence of costly attacks by Australian divisions during the Somme campaign, where McDonald's compatriot, the sculptor Wallace Anderson, also saw action.[24]

78

Notes

1 AWM 1920. Australian War Memorial F00069.
2 Anderson 2012, pp. 62–3, 71.
3 Andrews 1993, pp. 56–7.
4 Pugsley 2004, pp. 29–32.
5 Anderson [n.d.].
6 In this respect, Anderson was complemented by another exhibit in the *Common Cause* exhibition, a Canadian Memorial Cross in memory of the Canadian infantryman Robert Bruce Holmes, named after the 14th-century King of Scotland (National Museums Scotland M.1993.825).
7 Anderson [n.d.], pp. 10–11.
8 Anderson [n.d.], p. 34.
9 Bean 1916.
10 Bean (ed.) 1921–42.
11 Anderson [n.d.], p. 62.
12 Anderson 2012, pp. 244–9.
13 Ken Scarlett, 'Anderson, William Wallace (1888–1975)', in Ritchie (ed.) 1993, pp. 54–5.
14 Anderson [n.d.], pp. 56, 65.
15 Dennis, Grey, Morris, Prior with Connor (eds) 1995, p. 552.
16 *Ibid.*, pp. 503–4.
17 A. J. Hill, 'MacLagan, Ewen George (1948)', in Serle (ed.) 1988, pp. 616–8.
18 Travers 2001, pp. 71–2.
19 Pugsley, *The Anzac Experience*, 269–70.
20 Grey 1999, p. 103.
21 Andrews 1993, pp. 172–3, 188.
22 *Ibid.*, pp. 156–7.
23 As a senior non-commissioned officer in the New South Wales Scottish, McDonald is likely to have had many dealings with the regiment's adjutant between 1901 and 1904, E. G. Sinclair-MacLagan.
24 Information about Captain W. T. McDonald from the online catalogue of the Australian War Memorial and courtesy of Craig Tibbitts, Senior Curator, Official and Private Records, Australian War Memorial.

Bibliography

Anderson, Nola 2012. *Australian War Memorial. Treasures from a Century of Collecting* (Crows Nest).

Anderson, W. Wallace [n.d.]. 'Autobiography': type-script copy held by the State Library of Victoria, MS12804, BOX 3574/3.

Andrews, E.M. 1993, *The ANZAC Illusion: Anglo-Australian Relations during World War 1* (Cambridge).

Australian War Memorial [AWM] 1920. *With the Dardanelles Expedition: Heroes of Gallipoli* Australian War Memorial F00069.

Bean, C. E. W. 1916. *The ANZAC Book* (London).

Bean, C. E. W. (ed.) 1921–42. *The Official History of Australia in the War of 1914–1918*, 6 vols (Sydney).

Dennis, Peter, Jeffrey Grey, Ewan Morris, Robin Prior with John Connor (eds) 1995. *The Oxford Companion to Australian Military History* (Melbourne).

Grey, Jeffrey 1999. *A Military History of Australia* (Cambridge).

Pugsley, Christopher [2004]. *The ANZAC Experience. New Zealand, Australia and Empire in the First World War* (Auckland).

Ritchie, John (ed.) 1993. *Australian Dictionary of Biography, vol. 13, 1940–1980* (Melbourne).

Serle, Geoffrey (ed.) 1988. *Australian Dictionary of Biography, Vol. 11, 1891–1931* (Melbourne).

Travers, Tim 2001. *Gallipoli 1915* (Stroud).

Featured objects

Defence of ANZAC, bronze sculpture by Wallace Anderson, 1933. On loan from the Australian War Memorial, National Museums Scotland loan no. IL.2013.16 AWMART 13664.

Slouch hat from the uniform of Major E.G. Sinclair-MacLagan, Commanding 4th Division, Australian Imperial Force, 1918. National Museums Scotland acc. no. M.2004.65.4.

South Africans

The springbok 'Nancy', mascot of the

4TH SOUTH AFRICAN INFANTRY (SOUTH AFRICAN SCOTTISH), 1915–18

THE PRACTICE OF ADOPTING ANIMAL MASCOTS IS widespread in military culture and has been known in British regimental traditions since at least as early as the eighteenth century. In an early manifestation of emigrant Scottish military culture in South Africa, an animal mascot played its symbolic part in proceedings when the part-time volunteer soldiers of the Cape Town Highlanders marched behind 'Donald', a Scottish highland stag imported and presented by the shipping magnate Sir Donald Currie in 1887 for the purpose of completing the unit's flamboyantly Scottish parade appearance.[1] The springbok doe 'Nancy', which paraded at the head of Great War volunteers, was more of a South African export however. When, in 1915, the Scottish battalion of the newly raised South African Brigade departed on overseas service, they took with them this mascot supplied by a well-wisher, a David McLaren Kennedy, who farmed in the Orange Free State. The living gift was accompanied by a message of support in lines of Scots doggerel verse commencing …

Hey Jock! Am sendin' ye ma 'Nancy',
An' hope that she may tak' yer fancy!

It seems likely that, in naming the animal 'Nancy', the versifier was inspired by the paramour of a rather more distinguished Scots poet, Robert Burns, the Nancy immortalised in his *Ae Fond Kiss*.[2]

The 4th South African Infantry came into being as a Scottish battalion at the agency of Sir William Dalrymple, an emigrant Scot from

Stirlingshire who had risen to wealth and influence as a director of multiple mining enterprises in the Witwatersrand gold-fields of the Transvaal. As a young man Dalrymple saw active service in the South African War as a volunteer with the new Scottish Horse mounted unit. While amassing his fortune in mining thereafter, he managed to continue his military pursuits as a founding figure of the Transvaal Scottish, a volunteer regiment which in due course became part of the permanent Union Defence Force.

In 1915, with the backing of the Caledonian societies of South Africa, Dalrymple's influence ensured the agreement of the Union government that one of the overseas service battalions of its new South African Brigade would be Scottish in identity. This distinction came with a price, since if the venture was to live up to the traditional ideal the dress and accoutrements by which Scottish soldiers were recognised internationally had to be organised. While the recruits were assembling, drilling and preparing for departure, it was through gifts from patriotic well-wishers that their battalion's Scottish cultural credentials were confirmed. A regimental Pipes and Drums was established when 13 sets of bagpipes, with an added gift of horsehair sporrans for the pipers, were presented to the battalion by another patriotic admirer of means, Mr William Dewar. Kilts were to be issued on arrival in Britain, thanks to the lobbying of the British Army's Quartermaster-General by Dalrymple and a fellow officer of the Transvaal Scottish.[3] Khaki 'Tam o' Shanter' bonnets came a little later, issued from British military stores when the battalion was set to embark from England for France and the Western Front. These replaced traditional Scottish blue

Below:

Men of the 4th South African Infantry at Carnoy Valley, the day after coming out of the Delville Wood, July 1916.

SA Department of Defence Documentation Centre

'balmoral' bonnets with red and white diced bands, which the battalion had already acquired, and the khaki sun helmets which had been worn by the men of the Brigade during its first operational deployment against Ottoman forces in the North African desert.[4]

The springbok Nancy was a counter-balance to all this Scottish regalia. As a living symbol of the fauna of South Africa, the animal was a reminder that, as well as being Scottish, the battalion was carrying overseas the national and imperial identity of the South African Brigade. It was the intention of the Dominion government that the Brigade should promote the reputation of the Union of South Africa, which it envisaged according to the imperial ideal of a united white nation. The use of 'springbok' as a term to denote a white South African was derived from the social, school and sporting world of the white élites which controlled the new Dominion state. In its successful British tour of 1912–13, the South African rugby team had come to be identified in the British press as 'the Springboks'. More properly in their own imagination perhaps, the South African rugby players were 'Springbokken', since the team, like the game, was an area where Afrikaners were as fully involved as their English-speaking middle-class counterparts, and would soon be in the ascendancy.[5] In this respect indeed, the springbok image appealed to the Dominion government, keen to encourage a national political and cultural accommodation between English and Afrikaans speakers. The official military insignia of the Union, worn by the South African Brigade as its cap badge, was the emblem of the springbok, with a motto 'Union is Strength' inclusively rendered in Afrikaans as well as English. The 4th South African Infantry wore theirs on a tartan patch. South African soldiers serving on the Western Front came to be known collectively and individually as 'springboks' by those serving around them, as well as in their own self-image.

Besides Nancy, there was a second mascot within the brigade – a baboon named 'Jackie' adopted by the Brigade's 3rd Battalion. As another animal native to South Africa, it performed a similar symbolic function. Both springbok and baboon were much photographed and publicised in the deliberate promotion of the South African presence in France. For the Scots, Nancy was an emblem signifying to onlookers that these apparently Scottish soldiers were a hybrid. The animal's presence amidst the kilts and pipes, and sometimes decked in a tartan coat, embodied a fusion of identities wherein the hardy, warlike Scot of tradition was revitalised by the vigour and adventurous frontier spirit associated with the imperial settlement of Africa. Like their fellows across the whole of the South African Brigade, the men of the Scottish battalion were also given to appropriating a form of black African identity by performing their versions of Zulu war dances and

Above:

4th South African Infantry
dance at Rouen, June 1918.

Ditson National Museum of
Military History

war cries.[6] One photograph of an informal display of this kind, taken
at the Bull Run training area at Rouen in June 1918, presents an extraordinary mixture of imagery as men in kilts and bonnets perform their
interpretation of an African tribal dance.

The celebrity attained by the springbok as a focal point for the
battalion's identity owed much to the novelty of its appearance and
behaviour in an incongruous setting. It was a star attraction when the
Brigade received a Royal Inspection by Queen Mary at the Bordon
camp training depot in Hampshire in December 1915. Nancy was
again prominent in the battalion's arrival on French soil in spring 1916,
greeted by the curious and enthusiastic populace of Marseilles who
had never before seen South African soldiers, or indeed kilted soldiers
of any description. Remarkably, the delicate animal survived the ensuing two and a half years in the alien environment of the Western
Front in the care of her keeper, Private Petersen. When the troops went
up to the front-line trenches, Nancy remained in rear areas behind the
line. Safety was not assured even at this distance, however, and Nancy
sustained an honourable wound when enemy shelling at Armentières
in 1917 caused the panicked springbok to run into a wall, damaging
one of her horns which thereafter grew out of shape. This irregularity
may be observed today in 'Nancy' as preserved after the war.

The springbok's formal role as a parade mascot reached its height
in a symbolically loaded moment for the South African Brigade in

February 1918. During a spell out of the front line, elements of the Brigade returned in pilgrimage to the scene of the Delville Wood action of July 1916 where it had lost so many men during the Somme offensive. The shocking casualty returns, and press reports of South Africans gallantly fighting to gain and hold the wood amidst dreadful carnage, had already made Delville Wood a focus of public mourning and pride for South Africans at home. Indeed, it is argued, public memory of the battle was being deliberately employed as a symbol of common sacrifice between Afrikaner and Briton to encourage a sense of shared white nationhood.[7] In front of the official photographers and a film crew, Nancy was prominent in a service of remembrance, which included a piper's lament and the erection of a wooden cross above the many small personal memorials already in place. This commemorative ritual within the Brigade pre-figured the Union government's post-war acquisition of the battlefield as the site of its South African national memorial.

The Brigade's war was far from over at this point. Further trials awaited the South Africans in the German spring offensive of 1918. Unlike many of the soldiers present at the Delville Wood memorial service in February, Nancy survived beyond the Armistice of 11th November. When the springbok succumbed soon afterwards to the privations of another winter on the Western Front, the affection and symbolic regard in which the mascot was held by the battalion was expressed in a military funeral and a marked grave. The story did not end there, however. In death Nancy continued to represent the national ideal she had embodied in life, repatriated as part of the heritage of the Scottish military community in South Africa. The springbok's skin had been removed and preserved before her burial and was sent to London for stuffing and mounting, so preserving the mascot as an artefact. 'Nancy' was from thence returned to South Africa for presentation to the battalion's father-figure Sir William Dalrymple, who gave it a place of honour in his mansion outside Johannesburg, a house he had named, with a nod to the Scottish highlands, 'Glenshiel'. Like the rest of the Brigade, the 4th South African Infantry disbanded and dispersed, but Dalrymple became Honorary Colonel of the Transvaal Scottish, which continued through and after the war as a Union Defence Force regiment. 'Nancy' became, in effect, regimental heritage, but with her broader symbolic significance in the history of the South African Brigade ultimately entered the collections of what is now the Ditsong National Museum of Military History in Johannesburg, originally constituted as a Great War memorial.

In today's democratic South Africa, the Museum seeks to represent the history and culture of all the elements of the modern South African National Defence Force, including the traditions of the white-dominated military forces during the colonial, Dominion, and Afrikaner nationalist *apartheid*, eras. It is with some complexity that Scottish identity fits into this shared inheritance, but it is notable that the tradition has survived all these changes. Units with Scottish traditions, with soldiers from a mixture of ethnic backgrounds, continue to serve the South African nation today. Placing the Scottish military tradition of the First World War into the contemporary picture is indeed even more complex than the task of reconciling African, British and Afrikaner military heritage might suggest. Scottish military identity in South Africa was rarely straightforward. In association with figures such as Dalrymple, the middle-class, empire loyalist character of the 4th South African Infantry might have enjoyed the unified support of Scots in South Africa and of most English-speaking South Africans during the years of the First World War. Historian Jonathan Hyslop has pointed out that the consensus did not last long. The first deployment of the Transvaal Scottish regiment after the war was in the violent disturbances of the 1922 strike in the Witwatersrand gold-field. With Scottish-born and Scottish-descended armed miners on the one hand, and with the Transvaal Scottish on the other, both sides in this deadly confrontation put out pipers at the head of their shows of force.[8]

Kilt

made for issue to the 4th South African Infantry
(South African Scottish), 1918

Since its formal inception within the eighteenth-century British army as the military dress of the new highland regiments, the kilt has carried a recognition factor which has made it the predominant material expression of Scottish military identity. In an ongoing interchange between civilian and military fashion, the kilt combined the traditional ideal of highland masculine and warrior prowess with the growing professional acumen and battlefield reputation of highland soldiers fighting the wars of the British empire. For a military unit of Scottish migrants in the late nineteenth and early twentieth century, the kilt, together with the bagpipes, was the obvious and ultimate signifier of belonging to that distinctive and prestigious military tradition. In Great War overseas service units, hastily assembled, the practicalities of kitting out a body of men with the kilt could be a troublesome matter. The support of influential patrons and well-wishers could be instrumental, which explains why this particular kilt of Murray of Atholl tartan, intended for use of the 4th South African Infantry, was for the best part of a century after the Great War stored with others in an attic room in Blair Castle in highland Perthshire, Scotland. It is stamped on its interior lining with the issue mark of the British War Office, and bears remnants of the 1918 issue label denoting the tartan as 'Transvaal Scottish'.

Formed around a core of volunteers from pre-war Scottish units of the Union Defence Force, the 4th South African Infantry was nevertheless lacking the full set of elements of a Scottish military uniform with which to display its chosen identity. The Transvaal Scottish and Cape Town Highlanders had departed for the 1914–15 campaign in German South-West Africa wearing their kilts of Murray and Gordon tartan respectively, but for overseas volunteers of the 'South African Scottish' there was no supply of either sufficient to clad them in the highland garb before they embarked for active service in Europe. Into the breach stepped a Scottish figure who had been associated with the South African military scene since his involvement in the war of 1899–1902. The Marquis of Tullibardine was heir to the Dukedom of Atholl, one of the great Scottish highland estates, with its seat at Blair Castle. Like several major landowners, he had been active in raising volunteer mounted units for the South African War, where he was already serving as a British army staff officer. His Scottish Horse mounted regiment had combined recruits from Scotland with volunteers from Australia and from within South Africa itself, who came forward at the urging of Caledonian societies and other networks of influential Scotsmen. With victory over the Boers eventually secured, Lord Tullibardine saw to the retention of Scottish Horse reserve units in Scotland and South Africa and also lent his support to the formation of the Transvaal Scottish as an infantry corps based in Johannesburg.[9]

In honour of his patronage as honorary colonel, and with that connection helping to secure requisite supply of the correct cloth, the Transvaal Scottish adopted highland uniform with the kilt of Lord Tullibardine's Murray of Atholl tartan.[10] At Tullibardine's behest, and with the permission of his father the Duke, this tartan was already being worn by pipers of the Scottish Horse. It had been worn for decades in Scotland by the Atholl Highlanders which, celebrated as 'the last remaining private army in Europe', was a ceremonial bodyguard of armed civilian retainers to the Duke, a rather fanciful notion at the outset but an enduring one that had emerged amid the fashionable revival and imagining of highland traditions in the middle decades of the nineteenth century. The design of this tartan, with a single red line added to the dark blue and green of the 'Government tartan' worn by the Black Watch, the oldest of the highland regiments of the British army, is believed to have originated with a regular British army regiment, the 77th Atholl Highlanders, raised by the 4th Duke in 1777 and disbanded in 1783.[11]

The 4th South African Infantry recruited for overseas service in 1915 was not one and the same thing as the Transvaal Scottish. But this distinction, which might have been uppermost in the minds of those of its volunteers who had joined from the Cape Town Highlanders and other units, was perhaps less than clear in the vision of Lord Tullibardine and the officers of the Transvaal Scottish who successfully lobbied the British military authorities to agree to supply the new battalion with highland uniform. When Tullibardine first reviewed the battalion, at Bordon on 15 November 1915, the officers and men had dispensed with their culturally unsatisfactory trousers, and paraded in the Murray of Atholl kilts with which they had just been issued. Photographs show the officers already equipped with the khaki drill cotton aprons which were worn over the kilt by British highland soldiers on active service, providing camouflage and protection for the expensive and water-absorbing tartan cloth.[12] The kilts remained in short supply; further drafts of men arriving at Bordon to reinforce the battalion on the Western Front had to wait to be issued with one. There was, however, a sufficient supply left over at the end of the war for the former Lord Tullibardine, who had succeeded his father as Duke of Atholl in 1917, to acquire a batch of army surplus kilts remaining from those earmarked for issue to the 4th South African Infantry in 1918. With these he intended to clothe his private retinue of Atholl Highlanders in future.[13] It was from this surplus supply that the kilt now in the military collection of the National Museums Scotland was acquired. In its rather prosaic link to the provision of highland ceremonial by the Atholl Highlanders at Blair Castle, it serves as a reminder that Scottish military identity, even on the bloody battlefields of the Great War, was in one sense the performance of an ideal, and a performance which required its essential costume and props.

Alexander 'Sandy' Grieve

A Personal Story

In the official history of the South African Brigade in the Great War, written by no less a literary figure than the Scottish novelist and historian John Buchan, Sandy Grieve is featured playing a piper's lament during the 1918 commemorative service held at Delville Wood.[14] Grieve, indeed, played 'Delville Wood', a lament of his own composition, and no more fitting or personal tribute could have been offered. Grieve was in the wood during the six days and five nights of July 1916 when the South African Brigade clung on to positions, which had been given names such as 'Princes Street' and 'Buchanan Street', against relentless artillery bombardment and infantry attacks. When relief finally came, and the shattered remnant of the South African Scottish battalion marched out of the wood, Pipe-Major Grieve and his pipe band led them away.[15]

Grieve was already a seasoned veteran.[16] Born in Scotland, at Largo in Fife in 1869, at the age of 18 he joined the British army as a professional soldier, serving as a piper in the 2nd Battalion Black Watch. When the South African War broke out in 1899, Grieve was recalled from the reserve for service. He was present with the Black Watch at the fateful battle of Magersfontein, where the Highland Brigade was defeated with heavy losses by the forces of the Boer Republics. Weeks later, in the British victory at the battle of Paardeberg, Grieve sustained a face wound which ended his war service, but only interrupted his

Left:

Sandy Grieve, front left, with the Pipes and Drums of the 4th South African Infantry, 1916.

SA Department of Defence Documentation Centre

piping career. He emigrated to South Africa in 1907 with his wife and teenage son. In 1915 he signed up for war service once more, joining the emigrant Scots of the 4th South African Infantry.

When Grieve played his lament at the Delville Wood service, he played upon a special set of pipes mounted in silver and ivory. These pipes, with a fine embroidered silk pipe banner, were a recent replacement. The battalion's instruments had lately been destroyed by shelling when left in store at Houdencourt in Belgium while the pipers and drummers were doing their front-line service as stretcher bearers and ammunition carriers. It was founding figure Sir William Dalrymple who, hearing of this unfortunate loss of essential Scottish cultural property, set about raising funds to re-equip all the battalion's pipers and drummers. As a flourish he procured the specially embellished set of pipes for presentation to the redoubtable pipe-major. The pipes are displayed today in the Transvaal Scottish regimental museum in Johannesburg, but it was in Cape Town that the Grieve family lived after the war, and it was with the Cape Town Highlanders that Grieve continued his reserve military service. His reputation as a piper only grew, and his leadership and tutoring of the Cape Town Highlanders pipe band earned for it the distinction of victory in the prestigious Chamber of Mines Trophy in 1935 and 1936.

When the Cape Town Highlanders mobilised for war once more in 1940, remarkably, Grieve accompanied his regiment on active service to the North African desert in 1941, until accepting in May 1942 that, at the age of 70, it was time for retirement.[17] As a piper, however, his career was far from finished, and on relocation to Bloemfontein, he formed and led the Bloemfontein Caledonian Pipe Band, still playing upon the silver mounted pipes presented to him on the Western Front in 1918, until the last years of his life in the late 1940s. When the pipes were sent to the Transvaal Scottish, his pipe banner was awarded annually for many years as a prize for piping at the Royal Scottish Gathering at Johannesburg.[18] The music of the bagpipes, and its martial connotations, is central to the Scottish emigrant cultural tradition, and its manifestation in South Africa was nowhere better represented than in the musical and military prowess of Pipe-Major Sandy Grieve.

92

Notes

1 Orpen 1970, pp. 6–7.
2 Kennedy's verse, and a response sent by Sergeant McBean, are quoted in Digby [1993], p. 24.
3 *Ibid.*, p. 19.
4 *Ibid.*, pp. 40, 82.
5 Hyam and Henshaw 2003, pp. 15–6.
6 Nasson, 'South Africans in Flanders: Le Zulu Blanc', in Liddle (ed.) 1997, pp. 292–304.
7 Nasson, 'Delville Wood and South African Great War Commemoration', February 2004, in *English Historical Review*, 119, 480, 57–86.
8 Jonathan Hyslop, 'Cape Town Highlanders, Transvaal Scottish: "Military Scottishness" and social power in nineteenth and twentieth century South Africa', *South African Historical Review* 2002, 96–114.
9 Campbell-Preston 1965, pp. 9–14.
10 Juta 1933, pp. 55–6.
11 Moncrieffe 1974, p. 7.
12 Photographs in the Transvaal Scottish regimental museum in Johannesburg and reproduced in Digby 1993, p. 41.
13 *Ibid.*, p. 40. The authors are grateful to Peter Digby, and to Jane Anderson, archivist at Blair Castle, for their advice about the provenance of the kilt.
14 Buchan 1920, p. 157.
15 Digby 1993, p. 135.
16 This brief account of Grieve's career is based on an unpublished paper researched and written by Sergeant Piper Rodney Muller, the regimental historian of the Cape Town Highlanders, and on copies of documents held in the regimental archives kindly supplied by Mr Muller to the authors.
17 Orpen 1970, p. 140.
18 Digby [1993], p. 351.

Bibliography

Buchan, John 1920. *The History of the South African Forces in France* (London).

Campbell-Preston, Lt. Col. R. M. T. 1965. *The Scottish Horse 1900–1956*, privately published at Fort William.

Digby, Peter 1993. *Pyramids and Poppies: The First SA Infantry Brigade in Libya, France and Flanders 1915–1919* (Ashanti).

Hyam, Ronald and Peter Henshaw 2003. *The Lion and the Springbok. Britain and South African since the Boer War* (Cambridge).

Juta, H. C. 1933. *The History of the Transvaal Scottish Regiment 1902–1932* (Johannesburg).

Liddle, Peter (ed.) 1997, *Passchendaele in Perspective: the Third Battle of Ypres* (London).

Moncrieffe of that Ilk, Bart., Sir Iain 1974. *The Story of the Atholl Highlanders* (Derby).

Orpen, Neil 1970. *The Cape Town Highlanders 1885–1970* (Cape Town).

Featured objects

'Nancy', the springbok mascot of the 4th South African Infantry (South African Scottish), 1915–18. On loan from Ditsong National Museum of Military History, National Museums Scotland loan number IL.2013.28

Kilt made for issue to the 4th South African Infantry (South African Scottish), 1918. National Museums Scotland acc. no. M.2014.4.

Victoria Cross
awarded to
James Crichton

2ND BATTALION AUCKLAND INFANTRY, 1918

PRIVATE JAMES CRICHTON WAS SERVING WITH THE
2nd Battalion, Auckland Infantry Regiment of the New Zealand
Expeditionary Force when on 30 September 1918, while crossing the
Scheldt River near the village of Crèvecoeur, he became involved in an
intense action which would see him being awarded this Victoria Cross.
The Victoria Cross (VC) is the highest decoration available to members
of the British and Commonwealth armed forces while engaged in active
service 'in the presence of the enemy'. Unlike many other decorations
it can be awarded to a service person of any rank in any branch of the
armed services. The design is simple, a cross pattée with lion and crown,
the words 'For Valour' and a red ribbon. There are no grades of award,
all are alike, and differ only in the inscriptions recording the recipient
and date of action on the reverse of the medal and its suspension bar.
The VC was first instituted by Royal Warrant on 29 January 1856. It
was originally said that the bronze from which all VC medals were cast
had been taken from two Russian cannons captured at the siege of
Sevastopol from 1854–55 during the Crimean War.[1]

The armed forces of New Zealand have had a long association
with the Victoria Cross. In January 1867 it was a New Zealander who
became the first member of a colonial force to be recommended for
the award. The original Royal Warrant had to be amended to allow
the recipient Captain Charles Heaphy of the Auckland Militia to be
successfully awarded his medal for gallantry in the first colonial New
Zealand War. The protracted correspondence and disagreement which
this recommendation provoked was, at one level, a bureaucratic dis-
pute over the exact meaning of the terms of eligibility given in the
Royal Warrant, which the War Office in London took to mean that
the decoration should normally only be awarded to members of the
Royal Navy and regular army. At another level, the New Zealand
Government's view that Heaphy was a soldier of the Queen, and that
members of colonial militia were, or should be, eligible, to receive the
highest gallantry decoration, was a point of honour in the relationship
between central and imperial government. The point was eventually
conceded at the centre in favour of good relations across the empire.[2]

This tradition of gallantry therefore stretches far back into New
Zealand's military history. Since it was first awarded, a total of 21
Victoria Crosses and one bar have been awarded to New Zealand
servicemen. With the outbreak of the South African War against the
Boer republics in 1899, New Zealand, as with the other Dominions,
came to the aid of Britain and sent a total of 10 contingents of volun-
teers which numbered over 6500 men. There was one recipient of the
VC from New Zealand in South Africa, the Wellington blacksmith
Farrier-Major William Hardham who had served with the fourth New

Zealand contingent. By this time, the Victoria Cross had acquired heightened status and popular recognition far beyond its original intention, and its stock has only risen since, to a reverence approaching cult status. Today, in common with other Commonwealth nations, New Zealand has its own honours system, but as with Canada and Australia, New Zealand retains the design and name of the Victoria Cross for its highest gallantry award.

During the Great War, the winning, awarding and conferring of the Victoria Cross was one signifier of the unity of the British empire, and a means of promoting publicly the sense of equality with which the war efforts of each Dominion were recognised. Public regard for individual recipients was something which government, press and people in New Zealand could identify with and take independent pride in, untrammeled by any sense of 'colonial' inferiority. These were the deeds of New Zealanders alone, reinforcing a growing sense of national military identity which, especially with the organisation of a New Zealand Division on the Western Front in 1916, could transcend the popular ANZAC image within which, since Gallipoli, they had been cast as the junior partner to the Australians.[3] James Crichton's award was one of eleven Victoria Crosses awarded to soldiers of the New Zealand Expeditionary Force. Seven New Zealanders who were serving in other Dominion or imperial forces during the First World War were also awarded the VC. This included three New Zealanders who were serving with the Australian Imperial Force (AIF), not however credited to New Zealand in any of the official records and statistics.[4]

In categorising James Crichton as a New Zealand Victoria Cross recipient of the Great War who epitomises Scottish emigration, it should be noted that this 'Scot' was born neither in Scotland nor New Zealand. James Crichton was born at Carrickfergus, County Antrim, Ireland on 15 July 1879 to an 'Ulster-Scots', or 'Scots Irish' family, the product of a transfer of people from Lowland Scotland to Ulster, which had its roots in the early seventeenth century. In turn many of these Ulster-Scots migrated to North America, where they became known as 'Scots Irish'. When James was an infant his family moved to Scotland, settling near Bathgate in West Lothian.[5] As was the case with many of the Ulster-Scots, James's family were strong Presbyterians. On leaving school Crichton had been keen to enlist in the army, but his ambitions were thwarted by the fact that, at five feet four inches, he proved to be two inches too short of the regulation height to join his chosen regiment, the Queen's Own Cameron Highlanders.

From the mid-nineteenth century onwards West Lothian became an important centre for both the Scottish shale and coal-mining industries, with many thousands being employed in these sectors and their

ancillary industries. After his disappointment at being turned down for military service it was unsurprising that Crichton ended up working 'down the pits' at a colliery at Northrig, West Lothian, situated close to his family home.

However, Crichton's desire to serve his country through army service was eventually satisfied in 1899 with the outbreak of the South African War between Britain and the Boer republics. Due to the demands of the war Crichton's relative lack of stature no longer remained a bar to his recruitment to the army. Thus Crichton successfully enlisted with the 2nd Battalion of the Queen's Own Cameron Highlanders on 13 October 1899. By the end of February in 1900 he was well on his way to front-line service in South Africa, as he was then recorded as being temporarily stationed at Gibraltar, Britain's military stronghold at the mouth of the Mediterranean Sea.[6]

Crichton served in the mounted infantry company of the 2nd Cameron Highlanders in South Africa through the entire course of the war until it ended in May 1902. He remained with the Cameron Highlanders after returning to Britain, and by October 1903 he had been transferred to the regiment's 1st Battalion. His army records reveal that towards the end of his regular military career his battalion's posting had taken him back to his native Ireland. His certificate of discharge and transfer to the Army Reserve, Cameron Highlanders was dated 23 January 1908 at Dublin. He remained on the army reserve list until 1911.

After leaving full-time military service he initially returned home to Scotland and to the coal mines. However, his return to mining was short-lived, and before long he was employed as a cable splicer helping to lay the section from Gretna Green to Glasgow of the new telegraph line from London. The early years of the twentieth century witnessed one of Britain's periodic highs in emigration levels. The dynamic of the new century's demographic phenomenon continued to increase with such intensity that by the years immediately prior to the outbreak of the Great War they had reached their 'greatest crescendo'.[7] As an unmarried, recently discharged soldier, Crichton's lack of personal ties made him an ideal candidate to become a part of this unprecedented exodus from Britain. By 1908 he had joined thousands of other young British men seeking new opportunities across the Atlantic Ocean in Canada. In September 1908 the army had granted him permission to remain in Canada while continuing as a member of the army reserve.

Crichton did not settle in Canada and within a few years he had set off for Australia, once again he remained there only very briefly, and by the outbreak of war the ever-mobile Crichton had moved on to Auckland, New Zealand. At the time of his enlistment in 1914 he was still working as a casual cable-splicer, having found employment with the New Zealand Post and Telegraph Department. Crichton remained unmarried, and as he started his war service he had to name as his next of kin his brother, who resided at Blackridge, a small mining town, west of Bathgate in West Lothian, close to where the family had first settled after leaving Carrickfergus.

Crichton enlisted in the 1st New Zealand Expeditionary Force on 22 August 1914 and embarked for Egypt in October of that year as member of the New Zealand Army Service Corps (NZASC). Crichton served in Gallipoli from October to December 1915, and then left for the Western Front France in April 1916, having by that time reached the rank of Company Quartermaster Sergeant. The NZASC was responsible for providing and maintaining all the supply services that a fighting force might require including transport, stores, clothing, motor workshops, fuel water and food. It was in the crucial role of feeding the troops in which Crichton was engaged as he served as a baker in the 1st NZ Field Bakery until May 1918.

Having had previous first-hand experience of direct engagement with the enemy during his time in South Africa, and with the hope of seeing action again, Crichton, who was almost 40 years old, took the decision to voluntarily relinquish his senior NCO rank with the NZASC. So in May 1918 he transferred to the 2nd Battalion Auckland Infantry Regiment as an ordinary private.

A mere four months after his transfer, Crichton was involved in the front-line fighting which he had felt compelled to seek. Thus it was through his actions near Crèvecoeur, France on 30 September 1918, during the advance of the New Zealand Division, that Crichton would be being awarded that highest accolade for gallantry in the face of the enemy – the Victoria Cross.[8]

The citation of the award appeared in the *London Gazette* on 15 November 1918, reading that Crichton had displayed the …

most conspicuous bravery and devotion to duty, when, although wounded in the foot, he continued with the advancing troops, despite difficult canal and river obstacles. When his platoon was subsequently

forced back by a counter-attack he succeeded in carrying a message which involved swimming a river and crossing an area swept by machine-gun fire, subsequently re-joining his platoon. Later he undertook on his own initiative to save a bridge which had been mined, and though under close fire of machine guns and snipers, he succeeded in removing the charges, returning with the fuses and detonators. Though suffering from a painful wound, he displayed the highest degree of valour and devotion to duty.[9]

It is difficult to imagine how terrifying this experience must have been, and to understand the level of pain which Crichton must have suffered throughout this exceptionally dangerous engagement. One fact not revealed by the official citation is that Crichton was initially wounded at seven o'clock that morning, and that he did not perform the last of his brave deeds until five o'clock that evening. A Nelson newspaper later reported that at the end of this experience Crichton had to walk six miles on his wounded foot to receive medical aid.[10] Another report told of Crichton's reluctance to seek medical help and that 'he was sent, under protest, to a field hospital.'[11]

A newspaper profile of Crichton published in 1927 threw light on his personality providing some insight into the way in which he acquitted himself on 30 September 1918 and also suggesting that Crichton was very comfortable in his acceptance of the national identity of Scotland, the most formative place of his four adopted homelands.

He was described therein as 'cool and modest' in a context which ascribed his character to the fact that he was 'a typical self-reliant Scot'.[12] It is interesting to note the extent of this codification of Crichton's sense of national identity, evidenced by the fact that even his enlistment papers note that he was also known as 'Scotty'. This identity would have been readily accepted in New Zealand. From 1861 onwards the Scots average level of emigration amounted to a quarter of all British migrants to New Zealand.[13] Indeed one historian has pointed out that at a time when the Scots made up about 10% of the population of the United Kingdom from 1851–71, in New Zealand during approximately the same period they were disproportionately 'over-represented', amounting to a figure of 30% of all British emigrants.[14]

In consequence the pre-war military organisation of New Zealand had featured a number of Scottish volunteer units, but these did not form the organisational basis of the New Zealand Expeditionary Force. The only national identity overtly evinced by the battalions of the wartime Auckland Infantry Regiment, including that of Crichton's 2nd Battalion formed in March 1916, was that of New Zealand itself. It may be instructive to note, however, the existence of photographic evidence from April 1918 indicating that the 16th (Waikato) Companies of the Auckland Infantry Regiment, recruited from one of the

Below:

The battle of Flers, 15–22 September 1918. Men of the 2nd Auckland Battalion.

© Imperial War Museum Q194

Above:

Pipes and drums of a
Waikato company of the
Auckland Regiment,
Louvencourt, April 1918.

**G-13177-1/2, Royal New
Zealand Returned Services'
Association Collection,
Alexander Turnbull Library,
Wellington, New Zealand**

pre-war Auckland Territorial regiments, had a pipe band at the
Western Front, with kilts provided by the Caledonian Societies of New
Zealand. In one image, kilted pipers pose with drummers wearing
standard service dress uniforms and the distinctive 'lemon squeezer'
hat of the New Zealand soldier which, demarcated in shape from Australia's equivalent 'slouch hat', similarly symbolised an ideal of the
pioneering outdoor spirit of the country.[15]

James Crichton returned to New Zealand in June 1919 and was
finally discharged in the September of that same year. Although his
period of military service was officially over due to the cessation of
hostilities, his military record also records a secondary reason for his
honourable discharge from the army, namely that he was 'no longer
physically fit on account of wounds received in action'.[16] Given the
description of the above action this is unsurprising. As one of the eleven
New Zealand servicemen awarded the ultimate accolade for gallantry
during the Great War, Crichton was feted as a national hero. Public
acclamation started with a civic reception in June 1914 on his return
from France welcoming him home to his adopted city of Auckland.[17]
In 1929 during a visit to New Zealand by the then Prince of Wales,
Crichton was one of the seven surviving VCs invited to a celebratory
dinner at Government House, Wellington, the official residence of the
Governor-General. A newspaper profile of Crichton made no secret of
the fact that the Dominion had 'adopted him both before and after the
war.'[18]

This public standing was to continue for most of Crichton's life, as almost 30 years later in 1958, at a reception for the King's Empire Veterans, Crichton attended as one of only two surviving New Zealand VCs. Time had evidently caught up with his other comrades. One newspaper account of this event recorded that when the toastmaster asked any veterans of the Second World War in attendance to identify themselves, this group of ex-servicemen was amazed when Crichton stood up. Unbeknown to most of his comrades for a short while in 1943 he had served with the merchant marine. A newspaper article from that year noted that Crichton was unable to attend a reception of the Auckland Returned Services Association with his fellow surviving VC holders due to his 'absence overseas'.[19]

Perhaps Crichton's greatest post-war public honour in recognition of his standing as one of New Zealand's VCs was the invitation he received to attend the Coronation of King George VI in May 1937. For this occasion he was granted the rank of Sergeant in New Zealand's Coronation Contingent. Newspaper reports from the time recorded that as the Contingent saluted their High Commissioner at New Zealand House in the Strand, the office staff of High Commission and other London-based New Zealanders 'shouted Maori war cries as they swung along'.[20] This form of identification with an interpretation of Maori culture assumed by the New Zealanders was an interesting parallel to the adoption of the 'Zulu warrior' image by the South African Brigade discussed elsewhere in this volume. The New Zealand Expeditionary Force had included Maori units in pioneer and other ancillary roles, but had denied full combatant status to Maori soldiers.[21]

Crichton had settled down to married life on his return from the Great War. His new wife, with whom he had two daughters Velda and Hazel, was a young English-born widow, Amy Watkins, whose first husband had also served with the Auckland Regiment and had been killed at Messines in 1917. Crichton's close brush with death in 1918 was an early episode in the long life he enjoyed. He died at Auckland on 22 September 1961 at the ripe old age of 82 years. James Crichton VC was buried in the Soldiers' Cemetery at Waikumete, near Auckland. His Victoria Cross and a collection of related objects and papers were presented to the Auckland War Memorial Museum by his two daughters.

Gold medal

presented as a tribute to Corporal James Sutherland
from the residents of Knapdale, Southland, New Zealand, *c.*1918

This small medal of 9-carat gold was an indication of the exceptionally high regard in which the people of Knapdale held those men from their locality who were serving overseas during the Great War. It shows an infantryman with rifle, and Sutherland's initials engraved into a shield above. On a scroll below is the motto 'For King and Country'. On the reverse is the inscription 'Presented to Corporal JR Sutherland by Knapdale Residents in Commemoration of his Services at the War, 14.6.18.' The tribute was posthumous and the medal was sent to his family in Scotland. James Ross Sutherland was an emigrant to New Zealand's South Island from Berriedale, Caithness, in the far north of Scotland. He had settled in Knapdale, a community situated just north of the town of Gore in an area of the province of Southland particularly noted for a heavy concentration of Scottish settlement. Such is the Scottish concentration in Southland, particularly round Gore and environs, there is a tradition that the phenomenon of the rolled 'R' in the local dialect is a linguistic legacy of the accents of the many Scots who settled there.[22]

Indeed the intensity of Scottish settlement in this part of the South Island is evidenced by a large concentration of place names of Scottish origin, including Knapdale itself.[23] The latter was named by Scottish-born Alex McNab after the place of his birth, an area of the Argyllshire west highlands. McNab had settled in New Zealand in the late nineteenth century to take up a major landholding in the district.[24] Given the number of Scots and those of Scottish descent who had settled in Southland this region would have been a logical choice as a new home for the young Sutherland. With its important pastoral economy, Sutherland could easily find employment in agriculture, having been brought up in the rural northern highlands of Scotland. On his enlistment in the army at the beginning of the war Sutherland was recorded as working as a farm hand.

Having volunteered for service, under New Zealand's Territorial system for organising recruits Sutherland was allotted to the 11th Reinforcements and added to the strength of the 2nd Battalion Otago Infantry Regiment, then stationed in Egypt following service at Gallipoli. He embarked from Wellington for Suez on 1 April 1916. After a period in Egypt, Sutherland and his unit departed for France; he then went on to serve on the Western Front until he was killed in action on 15 December 1917, aged 29 years. His death came just after the end of the Third Battle of Ypres, one of the most famous actions on the Western Front, more commonly known as Passchendaele. This battle is one of those engagements of the Great War which has become very closely associated with the New Zealanders and which still strikes a poignant chord in the national consciousness.

Sutherland had survived his battalion's experience in the first wave of the assault at Bellevue in early October, but was killed at time when elements of the New Zealand Division had been tasked to help strengthen the defences of this key sector of the front line. The New Zealanders had initially taken over this section during the heat of battle. A history of their service in the Great War describes the tense situation in which these improvements had to be made as there was a 'real and serious anticipation of a major enemy offensive.[25] The official history of the Otago Regiment records no casualties on 15 December, and it appears likely that Sutherland was one of those men of the 2nd Battalion who died after being wounded in a bombardment five days earlier.[26]

The community of Knapdale was clearly deeply affected by the service and sacrifice of their young men. Apart from the tribute medal presented posthumously to Sutherland, the community also produced a photographic montage showing the five 'Knapdale Boys', which of course included Sutherland, killed during the course of the Great War, an intimate and local commemoration of the losses borne by the families of this small rural township in the heart of the province of Southland.[27] This is in stark contrast to the national and imperial forms of memorialisation of Sutherland and his fallen comrades, including

the New Zealand Memorial, situated within the Buttes New British Cemetery, Zonnebeke, West-Vlaanderen, one of the many Commonwealth war cemeteries in Belgium. This memorial commemorates the 378 officers and men of the New Zealand Brigade who had no known grave, and who had been killed in and around the Polygon Wood sector of the Western Front between September 1917 and May 1918. Somewhat ironically the site upon which the cemetery now stands was formerly a military drill-ground.[28]

Sutherland's mother and father Ellen and John were residing at Braemore in Caithness at the time of their son's death in 1917. As Sutherland was British-born his parents received one the Memorial plaques which were sent to the next of kin of all the British dead after the war. These were issued by the British government, on behalf of the King, and due to both their colour and shape they became more commonly, if rather chillingly, known as the 'Dead Man's Penny'. Born in Scotland, and of Scottish parentage, this New Zealand soldier's name was also added to the names of the dead commemorated at the Scottish National War Memorial in Edinburgh Castle.

James was the youngest of the Sutherland family's three sons. It was common, though not exclusively the case, that the younger sons of rural-dwelling Scottish families chose emigration as a way of advancing their prospects.[29] Sutherland also had a young nephew called Donald Ross, who had served as a Territorial Force part-time soldier with the Lovat Scouts, a mounted regiment which recruited in the highlands of Scotland.[30] Donald was the illegitimate son of James's older sister Isabella, who had been brought up in the Sutherland family home. The 1901 census return had been altered to suggest that Donald was actually the son, and not a grandson of the Sutherlands. Donald never saw service at the front, and died at home in February 1917. As he was still an enlisted serviceman at the time of his death, he too is 'remembered with honour'. His remains rest at the Braemore Burial Ground, at Latheron, so much closer than those of his uncle to the Caithness family home.

Jock Sutherland

A Personal Story

Sutherland, affectionately known as Jock, was born on 14 November 1886 the son of David and Margaret Sutherland, a family with strong Scottish roots. Despite having the same fairly common Scottish surname, Jock's family was not related to James Sutherland above. At that time the Sutherlands were living in Dunedin, Otago; this city and its regional hinterland became a main destination for Scottish emigrants during that period of mass emigration to New Zealand which began in the mid-nineteenth century.[31]

Soon after the outbreak of the war, Sutherland was living in the small rural town of Waimate, in the south of Canterbury Province, where he found employment as a printer at the town's Progress Printing Works. Sutherland was actively involved in the town's Scottish associational life, becoming a well-respected member of the Waimate Pipe Band. The formation of pipe bands in New Zealand was a key element of Scottish associational culture, which possessed 'both ceremonial and entertainment purposes' for local communities such as Waimate.[32] Although the South Island Province of Canterbury and its provincial capital Christchurch had its origins in a settlement association, established in 1848, sponsored by the Church of England, it was also a popular destination for Scottish emigrants.[33] He and his band took part in in competitions, and Sutherland had medals, one dated 1910, which proved their musical prowess. One particularly prized award was the gold medal presented to Sutherland by the Waimate Pipe Band as 'a token of honour' for his service in the Great War'.[34]

In the years after the war Sutherland had moved to Christchurch, where was to spend most of his working life in the print shop of *The Press*, which was Canterbury's principal daily newspaper.

Only ten days after Britain declared war on Germany, Sutherland had already enlisted for

Below:

Jock and Helen on their wedding day, 1 January 1919.

Auckland War Memorial Museum – Tāmaki Paenga Hira PH-2007-7

active service.[35] He joined the 2nd South Canterbury Infantry Regiment, the unit of the NZEF which recruited for the existing territorial regiments in his part of the South Island's Canterbury province. However, Sutherland was one of the 'many officers and men who refer with pride to their association with the Canterbury Regiment, who have never had any service with the Territorials.'[36]

He left New Zealand on 6 October 1914, with the rest of the First Main Body, sailing initially to Egypt and then on, with the Canterbury Infantry Battalion which now formed part of the ANZAC forces, to the 'Balkans' theatre of war; this meant Gallipoli. Sutherland served in that costly campaign which saw so many casualties, including the commanding officer of Sutherland's battalion, Lieutenant-Colonel D. MacBean Stewart.[37] The Canterbury Battalion were drawn into many of the bitterest battles of the Gallipoli campaign, including the defence of the rather benign sounding 'Little' or 'Baby' Hill 700, so called because of its relative short height above sea-level.[38]

Sutherland was awarded the 1914–15 Star, which was issued to officers and men of British and Imperial forces who served in any theatre of the War between 5 August 1914 and 31 December 1915. He also received a Princess Mary Gift Box, with which all British Empire troops serving overseas in December 1914 were presented. Princess Mary was the only daughter of King George V. It was later issued to all troops who served on Gallipoli. This medal and the Princess Mary Gift Box, and other material relating to him and his son Ross, have been donated by his grandson to the Auckland War Memorial Museum.[39]

Having survived the Gallipoli campaign Sutherland returned briefly to Egypt. However, he was soon on his way with the rest of his comrades from New Zealand to the Western Front and further active service. Sutherland was promoted twice during the time of his war service, firstly to sergeant, and by the time the conflict had come to an

Right:

Princess Mary Gift Box, presented to all British Empire troops serving overseas in December 1914.

Sutherland Collection (1914), Auckland War Memorial Museum – Tāmaki Paenga Hira 2006.86.2

end he had been commissioned, attaining the rank of 2nd Lieutenant. More importantly for Sutherland, it was while he was stationed in Britain that he met, fell in love with and married Helen Clifford. Helen, who hailed from Somerset in the west country of England, was a lady's maid in Oxford, close to where Sutherland was stationed with his battalion after its return from the Western Front. Soon after their wedding ceremony on 1 January 1919, Helen embarked on the long voyage to New Zealand in the company of her new husband, as a Great War bride.

Around 1925 he moved, with Helen and their young son Ross, from South Canterbury to Christchurch, where he was to spend the rest of his working life in the print shops of the newspaper industry. Initially he worked for the *Lyttleton Times,* and after this title merged with *The Press,* Canterbury's principal daily newspaper, he continued to work at *The Press* until his retirement.[40] Family members have recollections of Sutherland and his 'classic bloke's shed that had jars and boxes of screws and nuts and nails and everything he never threw away – all meticulously labelled'.[41] His grandson believes 'that precision came from his printing experiences'.[42] It seems possible that when Sutherland enjoyed a smoke in that shed, he lit up with a match from his treasured *Thom & Cameron Highland Whiskies* matchbox, kept as a reminder of his war service and his links to Scotland.

The Sutherland family tradition of Commonwealth war service with a Scottish connection continued with Jock's son Ross during the Second World War. He enlisted with the New Zealand Scottish Regiment in 1940, eventually sailing on the *Aquitania* in 1942, for active service with the 27th (Machine Gun) Battalion, 2nd New Zealand Expeditionary Force in North Africa and Italy.[43]

Above:

Gold medal presented to Sutherland by the Waimate Pipe Band as 'a token of honour for his service in the Great War'.

Sutherland Collection (1919), Auckland War Memorial Museum – Tāmaki Paenga Hira 2006.86.6

Notes

1 Crook 1975, p 34.
2 The wrangling over this issue is set out in Crook 1975, pp. 149–55.
3 Pugsley 1998, pp. 27–9.
4 Peter Dennis and Jeffrey Grey, 'New Zealanders in the AIF: An introduction to the AIF Database Project', in Crawford and McGibbon (eds) 2007, p. 404.
5 The biographical details of Crichton's early life have been drawn from a number of unpublished sources kindly made available by the Auckland War Memorial Museum, including information supplied to the Museum by his daughters, Velda and Hazel Crichton.
6 The authors are grateful to Rose Young, Curator of History, Auckland War Memorial Museum, for the information from Crichton's service documentation on which this account is based.
7 Richards 2004, pp. 207–8.
8 The battalion's action at Crèvecouer is described in Burton 1921, pp. 250–5.
9 *London Gazette*, 15 November 1918.
10 *Colonist*, volume LXI, issue no. 15120, 10 July 1919, p. 3.
11 Harper and Richardson 2006, p. 66.
12 'The Coolness of Crichton' in *NZ Truth*, 16 June 1927, p. 4.
13 Bueltmann *et al.* 2013, p. 238.
14 Bueltmann 2011, p. 35.
15 Royal New Zealand Returned and Services Association Collection, Alexander Turnbull Library, National Library of New Zealand, G-13177-1/2.
16 Based on information sourced in the entry for Crichton in the Auckland War Memorial Museum's Cenotaph Database.
17 *Auckland Star*, 24 June 1919, p. 4.
18 *NZ Truth*, 16 June 1927, p. 4.
19 *New Zealand Herald*, 10 July 1943, n.p.
20 *The Singapore Free Press and Mercantile Advertiser*, 30 April 1937, p. 25.
21 Monty Soutar, 'Tee Hokowhitu-a-Tu: a Coming of Age?', in Crawford and McGibbon 2007, pp. 102–3.
22 Tom Brooking, 'Sharing out the Haggis: The special Scottish contribution to New Zealand history', in Brooking and Coleman (eds) 2003, p. 49; and Sharon Marsden, 'On the emergence of regional varieties of New Zealand English', in *New Zealand English Journal* 21, 2007, pp. 64–72.
23 Pearce 1976, pp. 172–4.
24 The authors are grateful to Seán Brosnahan, Curator of History, Otago Settlers Museum, Dunedin, for sourcing the provenance of Knapdale, Southland.
25 Stewart 1921, p. 316.
26 Byrne 1921, pp. 240–2.
27 National Museums Scotland acc. no. M.1993.95.3.
28 Ian McGibbon, *New Zealand Battlefields and Memorials of the Western Front*, Auckland, 2001, 25. Also information on the website of the Commonwealth War Graves Commission.
29 Devine 2006, pp. 482–3.
30 Donald had enlisted in the 3rd/1st Lovat Scouts, a regimental training unit raised at Beauly in July 1915. This body of the Lovat Scouts moved to Perth in June 1916 and was finally disbanded in January 1917.
31 Richards 2004, pp. 119 and 125.
32 Tom Brooking and Jennie Colman, 'Newest Scotland: life and leisure of Scottish immigrants in New Zealand to 1940', in Bethune (ed.) 1998, p. 14.
33 Tom Brooking, 'Sharing out the Haggis: The special Scottish contribution to New Zealand history', in Brooking and Coleman 2003, p. 50; Pearce 1976, p. 49.
34 Auckland War Memorial Museum acc. nos for 1910 2nd prize medal (2006.86.8); presentational medal from Waimate Pipe Band for Sutherland's war service in the NZEF (2006.86.6).
35 For Sutherland's service history, see: http://ndhadeliver.natlib.govt.nz/delivery/DeliveryManagerServlet?dps_pid=IE18725816
36 Ferguson 1921, p. 2.
37 Pugsley 2004, p. 88.
38 Pugsley 1998, p. 16.
39 Auckland War Memorial Museum: Princess Mary Gift Box, acc. no. 2006.86.2; 1914–1915 Star, acc. no. 2006.86.3. The authors are grateful to Rose Young, Curator of History, at the Auckland Museum, for help in identifying the Sutherland collection. His grandson, Brent Sutherland, has been an invaluable source of both family history and photographs.
40 From *The Life and Times of Ross Sutherland*, a manuscript of family history prepared for Ross's funeral, based on a memoir written by him for a presentation to a Rotary Club.

41 Correspondence with Brent Sutherland, 3 May 2014.
42 As above.
43 *The Life and Times of Ross Sutherland;* and the Association Notes from the catalogue entries for Ross Sutherland in the Sutherland Collection, Auckland Museum.

Bibliography

Bethune, Norma J. (ed.) 1998. *Work 'n' Pastimes: 150 years of pain and pleasure labour and leisure* (Dunedin).

Brooking, Tom and Jennie Coleman (eds) 2003. *The Heather and the Fern: Scottish Migration and New Zealand Settlement* (Dunedin).

Bueltmann, Tanja 2011. *Scottish Ethnicity and the Making of New Zealand Society, 1850–1930* (Edinburgh).

Bueltmann, Tanja, Andrew Hinson and Graeme Morton 2013. *The Scottish Diaspora* (Edinburgh).

Burton, MM, 2/Lieut. O. E. 1921. *The Auckland Regiment* (Whitcombe & Tombs, Auckland).

Byrne, A. E. 1921. *Official History of the Otago Regiment, N.Z.E.F in the Great War 1914–1918* (Dunedin: Wilkie and Co.).

Crook, M. J. 1975. *The Evolution of the Victoria Cross* (Tunbridge Wells).

Crawford, John and Ian McGibbon (eds) 2007. *New Zealand's Great War. New Zealand, the Allies and the First World War* (Auckland).

Devine, Tom 2006. *The Scottish Nation (London)*.

David Ferguson, David 1921. *The History of the Canterbury Regiment, NZEF. 1914–1919* (Auckland).

Harper, Glyn and Colin Richardson 2006. *Best and Bravest: Kiwis awarded the Victoria Cross* (Auckland).

McGibbon, Ian 2001. *New Zealand Battlefields and Memorials of the Western Front* (Auckland).

Pearce, G. L. 1976. *The Scots in New Zealand*, (Auckland).

Pugsley, Christopher 1998. *Gallipoli: The New Zealand Story* (Auckland).

Pugsley, Christopher 2004. *The Anzac Experience: New Zealand, Australia and Empire in the First World War* (Auckland).

Richards, Eric 2004. *Britannia's Children: Emigration from England, Scotland, Wales and Ireland since 1600* (London and New York).

Stewart, H. 1921. *The New Zealand Division, 1916–1919: A Popular History based on Official Records* (Auckland).

Featured objects

Victoria Cross of Private James Crichton, on loan from Auckland War Memorial Museum – Tāmaki Paenga Hira. National Museums Scotland loan no. 2002.48.1.

Gold medal presented as a tribute to Corporal James Sutherland, National Museums Scotland acc. no. M.1993.95.1.

Anglo-Scots

Field Communion set of the Reverend D. C. Lusk, Chaplain

1ST BATTALION LONDON SCOTTISH, 1916–19

A MILITARY CHAPLAIN'S RESPONSIBILITIES FOR THE pastoral care of soldiers reached heightened levels of intensity in the theatre of war. To the ongoing duties of leading regular services of worship, and the offering of individual spiritual and emotional guidance, were added the requirement to minister to the wounded and dying on the field of battle itself, and the frequent call to preside over burials. For this reason, an essential piece of equipment for the military chaplain was a portable communion set, where the miniature chalice, paten and wine bottle could be packed away with the wafer box and communion cloths into a small leather carrying case. Sets of this kind were in use among chaplains, travelling clergymen and missionaries in peacetime. They were advertised for sale privately and, for military chaplains, were available as War Office issue. The communion set used on the Western Front by the Reverend D. C. Lusk is typical of the latter, being ecumenical and utilitarian in design. But in one respect it is distinctive. It includes a large cloth embroidered in each corner with the regimental badge of the London Scottish, replete with Scottish heraldry in its central Lion Rampant device, saltire and thistles.[1]

Facing the possibility of imminent death, it was not every soldier who turned to religion. The chaplain, or padre, however, was an officer whose presence was usually welcomed, and one who could earn the respect of the most hard-bitten of soldiers on the basis of his readiness to share the dangers of operating in the field of battle, despite being unarmed. The War Office demonstrated its understanding of the importance and contingency of this kind of respect when, in late 1915, it lifted its official ban on chaplains operating on the firing line, a restriction which had been unpopular and widely flouted.[2]

The Reverend Lusk could not be faulted on the score of accepting risk and hardship. He took over the acting chaplaincy of 1st Battalion London Scottish in August 1916, while the battle of the Somme was still raging, and quickly impressed with his coolness under fire for which he received a Mention in Despatches. More importantly perhaps, his conduct earned the regard and trust of the soldiers around him, one of whom wrote:

> He is a hero, and from what I saw on the Somme, he is the bravest man
> in our Battalion. God bless him! How he worked on the Somme,
> tending the wounded in the line, saying a short prayer over lads being
> buried in Leuze Wood when a barrage fire was at its worst! Day and
> night he worked. Always a smile, a kind word, a sympathetic manner.
> I guess he was as hungry, thirsty, tired and verminous as we were.[3]

This correspondent suggested that Lusk should have received the

Victoria Cross for his work at the Somme. Although the highest of all gallantry awards was not to be conferred upon him, Lusk was later twice decorated, with the Military Cross for gallantry in 1917 and with a Bar to the Military Cross in 1918, signifying a second award. Again, it was for tireless and unflinching devotion to duty, offering practical as well as spiritual succour to the wounded whilst under fire, that Lusk's bravery was recognised.

Clearly cut out by temperament for the military chaplain role, Lusk was also suited for ministering to the London Scottish by dint of his calling as a Presbyterian clergyman. Adherence to Scottish forms of religion was one element of difference which distinguished the cultures of the Scottish regiments of the British army, where in chaplaincy matters the mainstream was Anglican. Despite being the established national church, the Church of Scotland had been required to lobby during the middle decades of the nineteenth century for Presbyterian chaplains to be recognised by the army on an equal footing.[4] While the recruitment profile of the different Scottish regiments of the regular army could reflect varying degrees of adherence to different churches, a Presbyterian chaplain was the established norm and appointed to each. The Church of Scotland continued to assert Presbyterian representation in the chaplaincy establishment of the Territorial Force and in the wartime expansion of chaplaincy work and appointments.[5] As part of the credentials of a Scottish regiment, and in its representation of a Scottish community in exile of sorts, 1st Battalion London Scottish carried a Presbyterian chaplain on its strength as a matter of course.

Established in 1859 as a rifle volunteer corps under the patronage of the Caledonian Society of London and the Highland Society of London, the London Scottish regiment was one of the most visible cultural manifestations of the Scottish presence in the metropolis. Unsurprisingly, the regiment developed a strong relationship with the Church of Scotland in London, another gathering point for resident Scots. A Scottish Presbyterian congregation had been meeting in London since not long after the extension of religious tolerance wrought by dynastic change in 1688, and the original Crown Court Church was established, flourishing in Covent Garden in the eighteenth century. In the late nineteenth century the size of the Scottish Presbyterian church-going community in central London outgrew the capacity of Crown Court. It was

Above:

Signed photograph of the Reverend D. C. Lusk wearing clerical collar and chest ribbon of the Military Cross and Bar, 1919.

therefore with the new St Columba's Church in Pont Street, which opened in 1884, further to the west, that the London Scottish Rifle Volunteers, headquartered in Westminster, established a close relationship. Both regiment and kirk were established in fashionable and expensive districts of central London, locations indicative of the prosperous backgrounds of those who were involved in the social networks surrounding each of the two institutions.[6]

By upbringing and education, David Lusk was entirely at home in the milieu of the London Scottish. A Territorial Force unit of this kind was, indeed, a metropolitan version of the social aspirations reflected in the Scottish emigrant regiments of the wider British empire. With the battalion's recruits drawn from among young employees in commerce, the professions and administrative work, former public school men and students, Lusk could expect to be ministering to his social peers throughout the ranks. In peacetime, a subscription fee, and the various expenses associated with maintaining the highland dress and its accoutrements, preserved a degree of exclusivity within the regiment. War service volunteers of a similar background were most welcome.

Born at Uddingston in Lanarkshire, Lusk had been a student at Glasgow High School and Balliol College, Oxford, before studying for the ministry of the United Free Church of Scotland. His calling had taken him to Jena and Madras before ordination as Minister at Innellan, Argyll, from where he returned to the University of Oxford to be

Presbyterian Chaplain at the new St Columba's Chapel. From Oxford that he accepted the military chaplaincy which took him to France with the 1st Battalion London Scottish from 1916 until demobilisation in March 1919.[7]

It was at St Columba's in Pont Street that a memorial service for the fallen of the London Scottish was held in October 1919. In the presence of Field Marshal the Earl Haig, the regiment's Honorary Colonel, and of other Scottish dignitaries, and with many bereaved families and comrades in the congregation, the Reverend Lusk addressed the service from the Gospel text St John 15: 13: 'Greater love hath no man than this, that a man lay down his life for his friends.' The opening words of his moving address recalled the occasions when his ministry was to the dead:

> *London Scottish, we endeavour to complete today those unnumbered solemn moments, when, in quiet places behind the lines, or under the starlight and 'under the arch of the guns', we laid to rest all that was mortal of our brothers, to rest 'in God's Keeping'.*[8]

The field communion set which did him such service in these years must have been for Lusk a precious and sobering reminder of these 'unnumbered solemn moments'. It resides now, with his decorations and other mementoes of his war service, and of a further ten years of service as peacetime chaplain to the London Scottish, in the regimental museum at the headquarters of the London Scottish in Horseferry Road.[9] The regiment continues in service today as an active British army reserve unit, albeit one reduced in scale to a single company of the London Regiment. The connection with St Columba's Church in Pont Street endures.

The communion set sits in the context of the present survey of the emigrant military tradition in the Great War as a reminder that military Scottishness was not solely about the flamboyance and spectacle of highland dress and piping, much as these aspects were enthusiastically embraced and performed by the London Scottish. Just as in places of Scottish settlement across the world, the unembellished forms and simple tenets of the Presbyterian churches in London were points of gathering and connection with the homeland. These were never more needed than in the years of war.

Leather purse

containing coins hit by a bullet when carried by
Private Harold Brierley,
15th Battalion Royal Scots, 1917

The arresting sight of a pay-book, cigarette case, New Testament or purse, carried in a soldier's uniform pocket and struck by an enemy bullet, is sometimes to be found in museum collections relating to the First World War. These artefacts are unsettling reminders of the arbitrary nature of life and death in combat in that war, whether they stand as indicators of the good fortune of a 'near thing' or, where they failed to stop or sufficiently slow the penetration of a bullet, as signifiers of a fatality. In the instance of the purse carried by Private Harold Brierley, fortune was with the owner, since Brierley survived the encounter with sudden death which it represents. Examination of the contents of the purse suggests that it was the loose change which saved him, or which at least preserved him from greater harm. Fused to the surface of these French coins, bent and twisted by the impact, are traces of lead, the remnants of an enemy bullet.

Brierley did not escape unscathed. He was reported missing on 28th April 1917, during the attack by the British 34th Division on the French village of Roeux and its chemical works. This was the second phase of Brierley's involvement in the battle of Arras, a British offensive in early April which had seen some considerable success in parts of the line in the opening phases, but which had since slowed against determined German resistance. The resumption of the advance in late April, with objectives including Roeux, was intended to take the pressure off French forces to the south, engaged in their own ill-fated Nivelle offensive. Serving with 15th Battalion Royal Scots, Brierley had been more fortunate than many in surviving the first phase of the battle, where the Battalion's losses had been heavy. The second phase was similarly costly. The 9th Battalion Royal Scots had already been repelled with heavy losses from the formidable defences around Roeux before the 15th and 16th Battalions of the same regiment tried again. Already reduced in strength to around 400 active men, Brierley's 15th Royal Scots sustained nearly 300 further casualties in the fighting on right of the attack line on 28 April.[10] Some 150–200 men in the forward companies were cut off from supporting companies held up behind them. With escape barred by the River Scarpe, and with the enemy counter-attacking in force, many of these men were captured.[11] Harold Brierley was one of those posted missing. His family waited anxious weeks for news, before receiving welcome word that their son was wounded and a prisoner of war in Belgium.[12]

The days and weeks after the battle of Arras were a trying time for a great many Scottish families. Such a concentration of Scottish units in the assault formations had not been seen since the battle of Loos in the autumn of 1915. At Arras the offensive was on an even greater scale. With two battalions of the Royal Scots heavily engaged at Roeux on 28 April, the losses from this particular attack were felt strongly in Edinburgh, home city of this oldest of the Scottish regiments and a source of many of the volunteers for its New Army battalions recruited in 1914, including the 15th and 16th battalions. But not only in Edinburgh, and not only in Scotland, because Harold Brierley was one of those recruits for the 15th Battalion who enlisted in Manchester, becoming part of a contingent from the north-west of England, known for a time as the 'Manchester Scottish', which formed around half of the battalion's original recruits. It was in Oldham, Lancashire, where Brierley had worked as a printer, that his family awaited news of his fate in spring 1917, as other local families in Manchester and its industrial hinterland endured similar torment, a delay which for others ended in confirmation of the worst.

Just as in areas of Scottish settlement across the British empire, it was the existing networks of Scottish associational culture which had brought the Manchester Scottish together. The Manchester Caledonian Association, founded in 1876, combined the customary social and philanthropic purposes of similar organisations worldwide, and in 1914 it joined forces with the Manchester St Andrew's Society to appeal

Above:

Private Harold Brierley, 15th Battalion Royal Scots, 1914.

© National Museums Scotland

for Scotsmen from Manchester and district, aged between 19 and 35 for what was advertised as 'The Manchester Scottish Battalion (Kitchener's Army)'.[13] The combined Scottish recruiting committee, galvanised by Sergeant Bruce Henderson, a former regular soldier with the Gordon Highlanders, was entering into a crowded field, as there was no shortage of recruiting activity in Manchester. Other committees were already engaged in filling New Army battalions for the Manchester Regiment, and concern was expressed amongst them over the entry of the Scottish effort into the field. The historian of the Manchester Scottish contingent has shown that there was confusion, and newspaper controversy, over whether it was ever the intention to create an entirely Scottish battalion to contribute to that local regiment, on the model of the Scottish Territorial Force battalions of London and Liverpool, or whether it was always envisaged that the Scottish recruits of Manchester might be despatched north to add to the strength of a battalion forming up in Scotland. But it was the latter course which was followed, with an agreement to send what amounted in the end to around 500 men to Edinburgh to join the new 1st City of Edinburgh Battalion of the Royal Scots, shortly afterwards designated the 15th Battalion.

While this apparent shortfall might seem to suggest an overambitious outlook for Scottish recruitment locally in Manchester, the overall recruiting picture was complex. Supply of enthusiastic potential recruits exceeded demand at times, and quality in age, health and build was a factor, to the extent that willing volunteers could find themselves turned away from army district recruiting offices and doing the rounds of the impromptu recruiting centres organised by the various local committees, including the Scottish offices in Market Street and Oxford Street. Forecasts of how many men the Royal Scots wanted from Manchester varied, and when the 15th Battalion was pronounced full, some initially disappointed Manchester men were passed on to join other battalions of the same regiment. Harold Brierley got into the Manchester Scottish contingent in October 1914, and it is noteworthy that there is no evidence to confirm that either he or his family had any previous connection to Scotland. It may be that there was something in his family or personal background suggesting a Scottish link or affinity, but it is equally possible that he chose to join the Manchester Scottish contingent because it was the readiest route into uniform that he could find, or because his friends were doing the same.

The Royal Scots were not alone as beneficiaries of recruiting activity in Manchester. With a more direct approach, recruiting parties from the King's Own Scottish Borderers had been there before them. The 6th Battalion Royal Scots tapped into the supply early in 1915 by opening a Manchester recruiting office. The 8th Battalion Argyll and Sutherland Highlanders, and recruiting parties from the Seaforth Highlanders and the Gordon Highlanders, were also active in the city.[14] There was no administrative bar to prevent Scottish battalions from taking men wherever they could find them, and in their recruiting efforts in the cities of the English north and midlands they would not have been overly particular about seeking Scottish credentials from those who were willing to sign up. Prior to the war, indeed, at least one Scottish Territorial Force battalion, the 6th Battalion Black Watch, maintained affiliated contingents of volunteers outside Scotland, in this case in the Irish cities of Belfast and Dublin.[15] Wartime recruiting in populous areas of England was simple pragmatism, but this was not, it seems, a practice which the Scottish regiments were overly keen to emphasise publicly at the time, or afterwards. The published war histories of the Royal Scots and other Scottish regiments, which tended to be focused on operations, made little reference to the somewhat cosmopolitan make-up of their battalions. The regimental rolls of honour in the Scottish National War Memorial in Edinburgh Castle must nevertheless contain an unquantifiable number of men, listed as the fallen of Scotland, whose first connection with the country might have occurred at the point of enlistment.

It was to Edinburgh Castle that the Manchester contingent for the Royal Scots departed in a series of detachments by train from Piccadilly station. Harold Brierley went with them, spending the winter of 1914–15 in barrack rooms in the Castle, training and marching to parade in one of the city's parks and attending church at St Giles. Public visibility to encourage army recruitment was part of the battalion's value for as long as it remained in the city. Before he left Edinburgh, like all of his new comrades, Brierley received a gift from the Corporation of the City of Edinburgh in the form of a pocket New Testament, embossed with the city crest on the cover.[16] More concerted training followed in four months at Troon, Ayrshire, before the battalion was concentrated with 34th Division at locations first in Yorkshire, then in Wiltshire, preparing for their part in the British Somme offensive of July 1916.

The 15th Battalion Royal Scots suffered badly in the attack at La Boiselle on the first day of the battle of the Somme, but Brierley emerged unscathed and was therefore in the front line again the following spring at the battle of Arras.

There is no documentary evidence to confirm that the wounds he sustained at Arras were immediately connected to the punctured and battered purse of coins which he kept as a souvenir of his war service. But family papers indicate that he suffered gunshot wounds to the

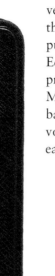

back, left hip and right foot, and it is highly likely that the purse saved him from greater harm that day, rather than on an earlier occasion.

Brierley remained a prisoner until repatriation in January 1919, and among the family collection of postcard photographs from Quedlinburg prisoner-of-war camp in Germany, one shows him convalescing in the hospital. It was to Oldham, not to Scotland, that the wounded veteran Brierley returned, and it was from Oldham that, much later, his family brought the bullet-punctured purse and the rest of the collection to Edinburgh. The talismanic purse was donated for preservation in the collections at the National War Museum in Edinburgh Castle, close to the former barrack rooms where this 'Manchester Scottish' volunteer from Lancashire spent some of his earliest days in military service.

Tom Easton

A Personal Story

Tom Easton was a Bedlington coal miner, born and bred in the English north-east county of Northumberland. Although Easton is a common surname in this part of England, it is also found in Scotland, perhaps an indication of much earlier cross-border migration. On the outbreak of the Great War, Easton enlisted with the 2nd Tyneside Scottish, one of four local Scottish battalions that would become part of the Northumberland Fusiliers. Perhaps it was less the recruiting cry of 'Scotland for ever' that resonated with him, more the proud claim that the Tyneside Scottish were 'Harder than Hammers' which drew Easton to this battalion.[17] This war-cry alluded to the heavy industry which dominated the economy of the North East.

Of the six large towns in England which had the highest proportion of Scots-born inhabitants, four were to be found in Northumberland.[18] The settlement pattern for Scottish migrants was that they tended to be found in the county's urban enclaves and from the 1840s onwards, as inward migrants to the county, they amounted to 'a sizeable group'.[19] With such a concentration of migrant Scots, the north-east was seen as a fertile recruiting ground for a military unit with a strong Scottish identity. Indeed there was already a Scottish military tradition within the county, which dated back to 1860 with the formation of Number 4 (Highland) Company of the 1st Newcastle Volunteer Corps.

The desire to form a Tyneside Scottish battalion grew in intensity in the weeks after the declaration of war, and soon the supporters of the plan took to the columns of the local press to advance their cause.[20] At the time of the South African War such appeals had fallen on deaf ears within the War Office. This time round, the need was greater and the campaign was driven by an energetic Tyneside Scottish committee chaired by Sir Thomas Oliver MD.[21] Oliver was an Ayrshire-born physician and a leading authority on industrial

Below:

Private Tom Easton, 2nd Battalion Tyneside Scottish.

Fusiliers Museum of Northumberland

123

health. As a Professor of Medicine in the medical school at Newcastle, he was a major figure in north-east public life and a leading light in the associational life of the city's Scottish community.[22] Oliver continued to be the honorary colonel of the Tyneside Scottish in the years after the Great War.

Whilst the proponents of a Tyneside Scottish battalion were unrelenting in their demands for official blessing, their constant petitioning of the War Office was ultimately aided and abetted by a decrease in flow of recruits around Tyneside. Finally in 12 October 1914, Sir Thomas confirmed to a meeting of his committee that he had received the necessary authority, including that of Lord Kitchener, to form the Tyneside Scottish. Very appropriately this news was delivered by Lord Haldane, the leading Scottish Liberal politician who, as Secretary of State for War, had presided over the creation of the Territorial Force in 1908. Announcing the formation of two new service battalions from Newcastle, Haldane stated that one of these 'might consist of Scots, who are my own countrymen.'[23]

As early as 19 October 1914 around 50 men had enlisted and optimism grew that the Tyneside Scots would soon exceed the required target of 1100 men to form a viable force of battalion strength.[24] At Christmas 1914, the members of the battalion were sent a message couched in the bombastic language of the era of the Great War, which exalted the 'fine body of men the Tyneside Scottish have secured'.[25] In a bid to ease and widen the process the focus of the recruitment campaign was extended beyond the bounds of Newcastle itself.[26] In November 1914 Easton would become part of this fine body of men, after he and his elder brother lied about their respective ages, each gaining a year in order to enable them to join the ranks of the rapidly increasing 2nd Battalion.[27] A mere eight days after the 1st Battalion had its full complement of men, the recruitment campaign had successfully raised a 2nd Battalion. In all it only took 28 days to form the Tyneside Scottish Brigade of four service battalions, a total of 4400 men.[28]

Easton was very proud of the newly acquired yet deeply felt traditions of his regiment. In his training notebook from his time in the field,

he took the time to write out a poem entitled 'The Lads from the North' which extolled the bravery of

> *... the Lads from Newcastle*
> *Who stood to their guns like men*
> *Who suffered and died like heroes*
> *In the battle of LA BOISELLE*

It was clear from this poem that Easton, as with many members of the Tyneside Scottish battalion who had little personal connection to Scotland, had no problem in adopting, and indeed promoting, a Scottish military identity.[29] The poem's final stanza exhorts the reader not to

> *... forget the Scots from N/C [Newcastle]*
> *Who have done what they set out to do*
> *And remember the price that has cost them*
> *To fight for King for Country and you ...*[30]

The action at La Boiselle referred to in the poem above was the engagement on the first day of the battle of the Somme on 1 July 1916.[31] The Brigade sustained over 2000 casualties that day and one notable fact reflecting the intensity of the losses was that the commanding officer of each of the four battalions of the Tyneside Scottish Brigade was killed in action as they led their men forward. Close to the scene of this battle today is the Tyneside Memorial Seat, unveiled in 1922 by former Allied Supreme Commander Marshal Foch, which commemorates both the Tyneside Scottish and their comrades in the Tyneside Irish Brigade, who, in similar style to the Scots, had filled four battalions of volunteers with Irish connections from the north-east of England.[32] This memorial is close to the famous Lochnagar Crater, the result of the detonation of explosives packed into a mine dug by Royal Engineers.

In a memoir recorded in the early 1980s by historian Lyn Macdonald, Easton recounted his experience of being in one of the mines whilst serving as his company's signaller.[33] After the massive detonation, some British soldiers received injuries from the debris as it fell back to the ground. Easton described the scene thus: 'You couldn't see much when the mine went up, but the noise was terrible. The fall-out was tremendous as well, but it fell short of us.'[34] Easton was also clearly well-practised in his skill as a signaller, as under very difficult circumstances he managed to maintain his company's 'link with the outside world' through a single telephone line that he had successfully connected.[35] And having a brother on the front line was constant worry for Easton. Towards the end of the Somme offensive, he suffered an agonising six days' wait to discover his brother's fate before finding out that he was safe.[36]

Easton had been promoted to the rank of corporal, had transferred to the 20th Battalion Northumberland Fusiliers (1st Tyneside Scottish), and was attached to a light trench mortar battery when he was awarded the Distinguished Conduct Medal for gallantry during the latter stages of the battle of Arras. The decoration was gazetted on 9 July 1917 with the citation:

For conspicuous gallantry and devotion to duty. The lever came off one of the shells and started the fuse action. He picked up the shell, carried it down the trench, and threw it over the parapet.[37]

Easton was captured in the summer of 1918 and was eventually held in a prisoner-of-war camp near Munster. In a letter sent to his parents in June 1918, despite his incarceration he was able to tell them that he had 'the pleasure once again to say I am keeping A1 and in fairly good spirits', though later in the letter he admitted that this was in part due to a recent receipt of a parcel of bread from the Red Cross.[38]

Easton never forgot the service, sacrifice and fraternity of his comrades of the Great War. He became an active member of the British Legion in his local area and a regular attendee at the many reunions held by the Tyneside Scottish Brigade, where he enjoyed the convivial company of his old comrades.[39] He was committed to the service of his wider community, standing for election as a councillor in local government in the North East, eventually becoming an Alderman. He also served as a Justice of the Peace. Easton was fiercely proud of his coal-mining roots and recounted his own experiences in the industry through recorded oral testimony.[40] He also committed to writing his memories of life in the North East prior to the War, and left a written record of his wartime experiences.[41]

When war broke out again in 1939, Easton served his country once more. As with many Great War veterans, second time round it was in his local Home Guard unit, in which he reached the rank of captain. At the time of his death in 1980, Tom Easton was the last surviving Great War veteran of the Tyneside Scottish association.

Below:

Colonel Sir Thomas Oliver carrying the Roll of Honour at the Laying Up of the Colours of 1st and 2nd Battalions Tyneside Scottish at the Scottish National War Memorial, June 1919.

Fusiliers Museum of Northumberland 6937.95/4

Notes

1 London Scottish Regimental Museum, acc. no. LSR0013.
2 Snape 2007, pp. 216–8.
3 *London Scottish Regimental Gazette* XXIII, 269, May 1918, p. 75.
4 Snape 2007, pp. 146–50.
5 *Ibid.*, pp. 181–2, 197–8.
6 The original St Columba's in Pont Street was destroyed by aerial bombing in 1941. The present church, on the same site, opened in 1955.
7 *London Scottish Regimental Gazette* XXIV, 281, May 1919, p. 69.
8 *London Scottish Regimental Gazette* XXIV, 288, December 1919, p. 181.
9 The authors are grateful to Andrew Parsons, Museum Curator and Archivist at London Scottish Headquarters, for information about the communion set and the career of the Reverend D. C. Lusk.
10 Paterson 2000, pp. 324–31.
11 Ewing 1925, pp. 423–7.
12 Dowson 2000, pp. 38–40
13 *Ibid.*, p. 5. Advertisement in the *Manchester Evening News*, September 1914, reproduced in Dowson 2000.
14 *Ibid.*, p. 12.
15 Ian Montgomery, 'Thoroughbred Irishmen: Black Watch Volunteers in Dublin before the First World War', in *The Irish Sword*, XXIX, 115, Summer 2013, 41–62. The authors are grateful to Allan Carswell for drawing their attention to this recruiting practice.
16 National Museums Scotland, acc. no. M.2001.37.8.
17 Both slogans appear on the same Tyneside Scottish recruiting poster, now in the collection of the Fusiliers Museum of Northumberland at Alnwick Castle: ALNFM:6308.
18 Bueltmann, Hinson and Morton 2013, p. 157.
19 John A. Burnett, '"Department of Help for Skint Scotsmen!": Associationalism Among Scots Migrants in the North East of England, *ca.* 1859–1939', in Bueltmann, Hinson and Morton 2009, p. 222.
20 Stewart and Sheen 1999, p. 27.
21 *Ibid.*, p. 26.
22 *Oxford Dictionary of National Biography*, entry on Sir Thomas Oliver: http://www.oxforddnb.com/view/printable/35308
23 Stewart and Sheen 1999, p. 28.
24 *Ibid.*, p. 30; and A. P. Whitehead, p. 1

25 *A Xmas Message to the Men of the Tyneside Scottish*, 1914. Fusiliers Museum of Northumberland: 6937/85.26.
26 Stewart and Sheen 1999, p. 30.
27 Whitehead 1947, pp. 1–2.
28 *Ibid.*, p. 1.
29 *Ibid.*
30 Tom Easton's Training Notebook, pp. 6–7. Fusiliers Museum of Northumberland 6937/15.
31 Macdonald 1983, pp. 73–4.
32 Sheen 1998.
33 Macdonald, p. 74.
34 *Ibid.*
35 *Ibid.*, p. 86.
36 *Ibid.*, p. 112.
37 *London Gazette*, 9 July 1917, Fusiliers Museum of Northumberland: 6937/5.5.
38 Tom Easton to his parents 29/6/18: Fusiliers Museum of Northumberland: 6937/85–37.
39 The Tom Easton collection in the Fusiliers Museum of Northumberland has a number of dinner menus and reunion programmes retained by Easton over the years, *inter alia* a Christmas reunion held on 4 December 1937: 6937/85.3.
40 Northumberland County Council T/40–2, Oral history recording of Alderman Tom Easton, 14 September and 5 October 1973.
41 Tyne and Wear Archives Service Tyne & Tweed, vol. 24, 'Life in West Sleekburn Colliery Village before 1914', by Alderman Tom Easton J.P., and Tom Easton Memoir, in Fusiliers Museum of Northumberland: 6937/85.35.

Bibliography

Bueltmann, Tanja, Andrew Hinson and Graeme Morton 2009. *Ties of Bluid* (Guelph).
Bueltmann, Tanja, Andrew Hinson and Graeme Morton 2013. *The Scottish Diaspora* (Edinburgh).
Dowson, Roger J. 2000. *Manchester Scottish: The Story of the Manchester Contingent of the 15th Battalion Royal Scots 1914–18 with a Record of Manchester and Salford Men who Served in the Regiment* (Manchester).
Ewing, Major John 1925. *The Royal Scots 1914–1919* (Edinburgh: Oliver & Boyd).
Macdonald, Lyn 1983. *Somme* (London).
Paterson, Lieutenant-Colonel Robert H. 2000. *Pontius Pilate's Bodyguard. A History of the First or the Royal Regiment of Foot The Royal Scots (The*

Royal Regiment), Volume One 1633–1918, (Edinburgh).

Snape, Michael 2007 The Royal Army Chaplains' Department, 1796–1953: Clergy Under Fire (Woodbridge).

Sheen, John 1998. Tyneside Irish. 24th, 25th, 26th & 27th (Service) Battalions of the Northumberland Fusiliers (Barnsley).

Stewart and Sheen 1999, Tyneside Scottish: 20th, 21st, 22nd and 23rd (Service) Battalions of the Northumberland Fusiliers (Barnsley).

Whitehead, A. P. 1947. The 1st Battalion Tyneside Scottish, the Black Watch, Royal Highland Regiment (n.p.).

Featured objects

Field communion set of the Reverend D. C. Lusk, Chaplain, 1st Battalion London Scottish, 1916–19. On loan from the Regimental Museum of the London Scottish. National Museums Scotland loan no. IL.2013.27.

Leather purse containing coins hit by a bullet when carried by Private Harold Brierley, 15th Battalion Royal Scots, 1917. National Museums Scotland acc. no. M.2001.37.1.

Global Scots

BEYOND THE BOUNDS OF THE MOST POPULOUS British Dominions, settlement, public service and private employment took Scots right across the globe.

Just as with Canada, Australia, New Zealand and South Africa, Scottish immigrants served in the expeditionary force of the British Dominion of Newfoundland.

In Asia and Africa, Scottish professional soldiers were already serving as officers in British imperial regiments when war broke out. In the major commercial centres Scottish associationalism thrived, and government administrators, men of business and employees of Scottish firms commonly became involved in local defence regiments, some of which displayed Scottish identity.

One of the main destinations for Scottish migrants through the nineteenth and early twentieth century of course lay outside the British empire. In 1914 many Scots resident in the United States of America responded to the outbreak of war in Europe by travelling home to join British forces. In 1918 they would be joined on the Western Front by Scotsmen and men of Scottish descent in the American Expeditionary Force. The Scottish American Memorial in Edinburgh's Princes Street Gardens, unveiled by the United States' Ambassador in 1927, was installed as a lasting tribute to Scotland's war effort and dead from the Scottish societies and prominent individuals of this powerful British ally.

From further afield in the New World, from the Scottish communities in centres of finance and maritime commerce such as Buenos Aires in Argentina, and from the cattle and sheep ranches of Latin America, young men also returned to Scotland to join up and in many cases to take up officers' commissions in Scottish regiments.[1]

This final chapter highlights a small selection of objects and stories to reflect just a few of these varied destinations and experiences.

Opening page:

Men of the Newfoundland Regiment line the rail of the SS *Florizel* ready to depart from St John's, October 1914.

With courtesy of the Provincial Archives of Newfoundland and Labrador

Silver statuette

of the Newfoundland Memorial
at Beaumont Hamel on the Somme

This statuette of a stag caribou is a miniature replica of the famous Newfoundland Memorial at Beaumont Hamel on the Somme. The original monument is situated on land purchased by the Dominion of Newfoundland after the First World War as a national memorial, testament to the fact that, in terms of its experience of warfare, 'no other name means as much to Newfoundland as Beaumont Hamel'.[2] The monument overlooking the battlefield, commemorated and advertised the fact that Newfoundlanders were among the 100,000 or so British and Commonwealth soldiers who were involved on the first day of the battle of the Somme, 1 July 1916, and shared to the full the devastation suffered by the attacking infantry on that day, with 90% casualties in the Newfoundland Regiment in only 30 minutes of action.[3] The statuette was made 40 years later by Garrard & Co Ltd, London, as a piece of military presentation silver. An inscription on the base records its presentation 'to the Officers of The Royal Scots (The Royal Regiment) by the Royal Newfoundland Regiment on the occasion of our alliance November 18, 1957'. The formal presentation took place at a ceremony held at Glencorse Barracks near Edinburgh, in September 1959 to mark this alliance between a regular Scottish regiment of the British army and what was, by then, a regiment of the Canadian Militia. This act of affiliation did not represent, ostensibly, an altogether obvious cultural connection. The Royal Newfoundland Regiment was not, and had never been, Scottish in its identity. Newfoundland was not traditionally one of the areas of present-day Canada, such as the provinces of Nova Scotia or Ontario, which had undergone intense levels of Scottish immigration.[4] But as a British colony, Newfoundland had experienced some degree of Scottish settlement from the late eighteenth century onwards. Indeed, Scots became evident at the forefront of Newfoundland public life, particularly in the leadership of the colonial reform movement of the early nineteenth century.[5]

Below:

Silver statuette of the Newfoundland Memorial presented to the Royal Scots, 1957.

© National Museums Scotland / On loan from the Museum of The Royal Scots (The Royal Regiment) at Edinburgh Castle

As signified by the presentation statuette, the military connection between Newfoundland and Scotland owed much to the circumstances of the Great War. Having crossed the Atlantic, and before heading off to the Western Front, the Newfoundland Regiment was stationed in various camps around Scotland. It was during this period, between February and May 1915, that they became the 'first overseas unit to be given the honour of garrisoning Edinburgh Castle'.[6] The memory of this distinction, and the comradeship between the Newfoundlanders and the Royal Scots forged in battle thereafter at Gallipoli and on the Western Front, helped to seal the approval of the alliance between the two regiments in November 1957.[7] The formal affiliation brought together the oldest British infantry regiment – with its roots as a Royal regiment in the seventeenth century – with a Commonwealth regiment enjoying the unique distinction of having the 'Royal' title conferred upon it during the Great War, in September 1917. The Royal Newfoundland Regiment traced its origins to 1775, on which history it staked its claim as the oldest regiment in Canada and therefore, again, a suitable partner for the Royal Scots.

Affiliations between regiments of the British army and overseas regiments from the Dominions was far from an exclusively Scottish practice, but it was one with which Scottish regiments had engaged enthusiastically since encountering colonial volunteer service contingents during the South African War of 1899–1902. While in these earliest days, the practice implied a sense of adoption by a 'parent' British regular regiment, and so a form of legitimation and recognition for the overseas part-timers, it was also inherently a mark of mutual respect based on the shared experience of active service. In this case, the battle honours won by the Newfoundlanders during the Great War are inscribed on the base of the statuette, emphasising that the Royal Newfoundland Regiment need not feel the junior partner in this essential regard. Success, endurance and sacrifice on the battlefield was the basis on which Dominion units had earned formal recognition and lasting friendship from the famous Scottish regiments they had once sought to emulate.

When Britain declared war on Germany in 1914, Newfoundland was a self-governing Dominion in its own right and it would be another 33 years before it became part of its larger neighbour, Canada. Newfoundland's constitutional relationship with Britain was therefore the same as that of Canada, South Africa, Australia and New Zealand. Although Newfoundland's population was a mere fraction of the size of the other Dominions, its government was no less committed to the cause of the war effort against Germany and its allies. And as elsewhere in the Dominions, this sense of patriotism was not limited to the political classes; it permeated throughout Newfoundland society. In a matter of days after the government had pledged its initial support for the mother country, a Newfoundland Patriotic Association was founded to lead on the great task of 'the raising, equipping and shipping of troops for the war effort in Europe'.[8] Newfoundland possessed a small, highly regarded Royal Naval Reserve, but this was its sole service body. There was neither a militia nor territorial reserve; the Dominion's military organisation was limited to a small number of cadet corps, which had been raised by each of Newfoundland's main Christian denominations.[9]

The success of the Patriotic Association's recruitment campaign, and the high level of public support for the war, was such that within days of the commencement of enlistment on 22 August the Newfoundlanders had raised their first contingent of the requisite number of five hundred fighting men. This initial body of Newfoundland soldiers would sail to Britain in the small passenger steamer the SS *Florizel*, part of the large convoy formed by the ships carrying their equally enthusiastic comrades of the first Canadian contingent in October 1914.[10] Such a rapidly successful recruitment campaign was no mean feat for a country with a population of only 250,000.

Geographic and cultural proximity to their Canadian comrades made the Newfoundlanders only too aware of their separate identity, especially once the Dominion troops were camped together at Aldershot, Hampshire. Indeed this desire for separate recognition was for a brief time reflected in their dress, through the adoption of distinctive blue puttees (strips of cloth bound around the leg from ankle to knee) as opposed to the regulation khaki-coloured puttees worn by the other imperial troops. This was originally a matter of improvisation required by shortage of the requisite khaki puttees, but the idea stuck long after the issue problem was solved. In much the same way as Scots were sometimes referred to in North America as 'kilties', based on that distinctive piece of their uniform, the original Newfoundland contingent soon became known by the epithet the 'Blue Puttees'.[11] 'Blue Puttee' also became a symbolic badge of honour for those Newfoundlanders who had sailed in the *Florizel* – the 'famous First Five Hundred' for overseas service, and a piece of military tradition unique to Newfoundland was born.[12]

Regardless of whether or not they were one of the First Contingent, when it came to national sensitivities all Newfoundlanders could be severely irritated when mistaken for Canadians during their time in England. In the years after the war, Captain J. E. J. Fox, a former Newfoundland officer, recalled that 'there was the fear that our identity would be lost with some Canadian unit .... we felt, quite properly, that if we were to give our best, we could only do so by pre-serving our own individuality'.[13]

It is impossible to be certain whether or not it was the strong New-foundland sense of national identity which oiled the decision-making process that sent them north to distant Fort George near Inverness in December 1914, but one commentator has suggested that this con-sideration may have informed the move.[14] Most annoyingly for the Newfoundlanders, having travelled all the way from Salisbury Plain, a further national solecism awaited them at their new barracks in Inverness-shire. As they made their final march through the gates, the resident band greeted the new arrivals with the strains of the then popular Canadian tune, *The Maple Leaf Forever* and not *The Banks of Newfoundland* which the 'Blue Puttees' would certainly have preferred.[15]

The memorial erected at Beaumont Hamel, with its defiant caribou in bronze by English sculptor Basil Gotto, was an emphatic statement of this feeling of difference, bound up within the prevailing urge to com-memorate there not only the 710 officers and men of the Newfound-land Regiment killed, wounded or missing in the attack on 1 July 1916, but also the total war losses from the Dominion of some 1500.[16] A caribou memorial of this design was placed in five Western Front sites sacred to Newfoundland memory of the war. And yet by the time the Beaumont Hamel memorial was unveiled by Earl Haig in 1925, the cost of the war and the post-war economic depression had put the fi-nances of the Dominion in a parlous state, which neither Britain nor Canada could ameliorate. The sequence of economic blows occa-sioned by the war would eventually lead to the loss of Newfoundland's separate Dominion status. The Great War traditions of the Royal Newfoundland Regiment would in due course become, if anything, more treasured as a result, as reminders of a distinc-tive past for this new Canadian province founded in 1949.[17]

Albeit at forty years remove, a formal affiliation, and an exchange of gifts, with as distinguished a Scot-tish regiment as the Royal Scots reinforced the sense of a unique heritage predicated on the service and sacrifice of the Great War. Scots might not have been predominant in the Royal Newfoundland Regiment, but as a regiment of the Canadian Militia the later generations of Newfoundlanders had not forgotten their wartime links with Scotland. In a ceremony at Edinburgh Castle in 1954, a plaque bearing the regi-

Below:

Plaque presented to the Governor of Edinburgh Castle to commemorate the Newfoundland Regiment garrison of 1915.

© National Museums Scotland

136

Left:

Lieutenant-Colonel Cluny Macpherson presents the Newfoundland Regiment plaque to the Governor of Edinburgh Castle, 1954.

© The Scotsman Publications Ltd

ment's caribou badge was presented to the Castle Governor and General Officer Commanding Scotland to commemorate the Newfoundland garrison of the Castle in 1915.

Representing Newfoundland at the event was the oldest surviving officer of that first overseas garrison who, appropriately enough for the occasion, was a medical officer with a self-evident familial connection with Scotland, one Lieutenant-Colonel Cluny Macpherson.[18] The plaque is preserved today in the military collections of National Museums Scotland. Meanwhile, the silver statuette of the Newfoundland Memorial at Beaumont Hamel has a permanent home in the Royal Scots Museum, Edinburgh Castle, marking a long-standing international friendship for a Scottish regiment whose Commonwealth affiliations also included the 10th Gurkha Rifles and the Canadian Scottish Regiment (Princess Mary's).

Plaid brooch

of an officer of the
Calcutta Scottish, 1914–20

This silver brooch, for wearing on the shoulder to fasten a tartan plaid, carries a distinctive combination of Scottish and imperial Indian heraldry. Superimposed upon the Saltire of St Andrew is the coat of arms of the Indian city of Calcutta, now Kolkata, all within a wreath of thistles entwined with the lotus flower symbolic of India. The brooch was made by the Calcutta jewellers and silversmiths Hamilton and Company, which also had branches at Bombay and Simla.[19]

Within the municipal arms, granted to the Corporation of Calcutta in 1896, are a ship under sail and sea-lion crest, representing the city's maritime trade and its late seventeenth-century origins as a post of the English East India Company. In 1914, the port and municipality of Calcutta was the nexus of trade and British imperial administration in Bengal. Inevitably, there was a concentration of Scots living and working there in the civil service, municipal administration, the professions, and in a range of commercial enterprises, especially in the export trades in tea and jute.

Scottish institutions emerged in the city in consequence to answering the habitual desire of these residents to maintain associational links with each other, and cultural links with a home, to which many always intended to return. As a reflection of the substantial Scottish presence, the rapid expansion of Calcutta during the nineteenth century as a financial, administrative and industrial centre saw the establishment of Scottish missionary institutions, churches and schools, the Scottish cemetery in Karaya Road, masonic lodges, and the growth of a Caledonian Society which sponsored the annual civic public ritual of St Andrew's Day. This celebration typically included a concert at the New Empire Theatre, which was a favourite with the young Scottish supervisors from the jute mill compounds concentrated along the River Hooghly.[20] For a more select experience, the Society hosted a formal dinner which at its height was attended by more than 300 guests.[21] From 1914, this important event in the social calendar of Calcutta was

Below:

Plaid brooch of an officer of the Calcutta Scottish, 1914–20, worn by Major C. H. Elmes.

National Museums Scotland

graced by the presence of men in a new military uniform. This silver plaid brooch was part of the highland full-dress uniform of another local Scottish institution founded that year, a part-time military unit formed as the Calcutta Scottish Volunteers.

The Calcutta Scottish was not directly a product of the outbreak of the Great War; its establishment pre-dated the international crisis by a matter of months, and the idea of kilted volunteer companies had been aired periodically over the preceding 20 years. The scheme which proved successful gained public expression in a series of meetings held at Calcutta Volunteer Headquarters in November and December 1913, and a 'smoking concert' and public meeting at the city's Theatre Royal.[22] The corps was inaugurated under the oversight of a committee of prominent Scots in the city, most of them senior civil servants and judges, and with the endorsement of the Governor of Bengal, Lord Carmichael, another Scot.[23] Fund-raising and recruiting among Scottish firms and leading citizens proceeded immediately, and more than a hundred volunteers were signed up within a week.

The aspiration was to form a permanent unit of the existing Indian Volunteer Force, which had been in existence as an auxiliary to the British Indian Army since the middle decades of the nineteenth century. The Force was, essentially, an auxiliary military organisation intended to defend the imperial establishment from internal threat, with roots dating back to the 'Indian Mutiny' of 1857–8. While the Indian Volunteer Force continued to fulfil thereafter the practical function of being prepared for active service in case of an emergency, service in a volunteer unit represented the expression of an ideal of public duty and civic participation implying élite status. Scottish involvement in the volunteer scene in the Indian empire and the British colonies of the Far East was a customary element of public social life. In administrative and commercial centres, where Scots were concentrated in sufficient numbers, and enjoyed influence with the military authorities, a unit or company expressing Scottish cultural difference through traditional military identity was a conventional aspiration.

By 1914, many units of the Indian Volunteer Force had attracted large numbers of Anglo-Indian recruits of mixed ancestry. These included volunteer companies formed by railway workers, at least one of which promulgated Scottish identity in its insignia.[24] This was not the outlook of the élite Scotsmen of Calcutta, however, whose liberality in the extension of honorary Scottish status extended only to laying membership open to 'Britishers' whose individual merit had been approved by the recruiting committee. Characteristically for those forming Scottish emigrant units, early deliberations of the committee were much concerned with matters of dress, and it was the idea of a kilted corps which had fired the imagination of the founders from the outset. The tartan chosen for kilt and plaid was the Hunting Stewart, which, as a notionally Royal tartan, implied no clan affiliation and was intended to be acceptable to all. The glengarry cap badge, the officers' sporrans, dirks, silver shoulder-belt plates and plaid brooches, acquired at individual expense, all carried the Calcutta municipal insignia to set off the traditional highland military effect.

The plaid brooch in the collections of National Museums Scotland forms part of the dress uniform of Major C. H. E. Elmes, who was surgeon to the Calcutta Scottish. As a middle-aged man in 1914, and with a frame from comfortable living, Elmes hardly presented a military figure. As surgeon, he was not required to meet the physical requirements for training and service demanded from active recruits. Elmes was, however, representative of the professional and social background of prominent Scots in Calcutta. As a student at Edinburgh, he had excelled in rugby and boxing before graduating in medicine and surgery in 1900. He immediately proceeded abroad to practise as a civil surgeon in the South African War. Moving on thereafter to private practice in India, he moved in élite social circles and was appointed surgeon to the Royal Calcutta Turf Club as well as to the Calcutta Scottish.

Below:

Major C. H. E. Elmes of the Calcutta Scottish, c.1920.

© National Museums Scotland

During the war, Elmes worked as a residency surgeon in Government service and was appointed port health officer of Calcutta, a post he held until 1923. His public and military service was recognised by the awards of a CBE and the Volunteer Decoration. Like much of the European population of a city such as Calcutta, Elmes was not a permanent migrant but a mobile professional, a 'sojourner'. He left in 1923 for a late marriage and his retirement at Cannes in France.[25]

Although technically liable for service overseas from August 1914, the Calcutta Scottish was never intended to go to war as a formed unit: throughout the Great War it remained in Calcutta in readiness for internal security duties should the need arise. One of its ancillary functions, in common with other units of the Volunteer Force, was to supply potential officers for regular units of the Indian Army which were contributing heavily to the British imperial war effort, and to the sacrifice of lives, on all the fighting fronts. It was the convention that Indian soldiers should be led by British officers, but with the multiple demands of

140

the war, and high casualty rates among junior officers in particular, there was quickly a chronic shortage of these.[26] For the enrolled volunteers who remained at home, which was the great majority, the volunteer ethos was temporarily overthrown by the demands of the war situation when the Indian Defence Force Act of 1917 introduced compulsory part-time military training for British males of military age. Units of the Indian Volunteer Force, including the Calcutta Scottish, provided the organisational basis for this form of conscripted service. As part of the Indian Defence Force, the unit was called out to deal with rioting in Calcutta in 1919, and was to be called out again after it reverted to its volunteer status the following year.

Post-war inter-communal tensions were harbingers of the end of British political control in India, and internal security would be the principal military focus of the unit's existence until its disbandment upon Indian independence in 1947.

In a manifestation of cultural affinity with another Scottish 'emigrant' regiment of similar pedigree, the precious King's and Regimental Colours of the Calcutta Scottish, the heraldic embodiment of the unit's service to the Crown, were passed on its disbandment first to the London Scottish, signifying a relationship which, in consequence of the transient nature of commercial emigration links back to London, had several former members in common. In 1951 the Colours were donated for preservation to the Scottish United Services Museum (now the National War Museum) in Edinburgh Castle.[27]

The Scotsmen who formed units such as the Calcutta Scottish were not permanent settlers in the manner of their counterparts in the British Dominions and would never have seen themselves as Indian. In the words of an Indian Volunteer veteran, a former Bombay Yeomanry Cavalryman from the days of the Indian Mutiny, addressing one of the Theatre Royal occasions intended to raise funds and recruits for the Calcutta Scottish, 'Most of us here tonight came out to this country to make money. There is no fault to find with that …'.[28] However, he enjoined that, in consequence, the young British men of Calcutta had a duty to contribute actively to the security of that imperial establishment which had made their pursuit of wealth possible. In the crisis of a world war, Scottish volunteer companies emerged not only in Calcutta, but also as part of volunteer corps in Bombay (now Mumbai), at Rangoon (now Yangon) in Burma and, further east, in the Chinese treaty port of Shanghai. Between these, and the Scottish company established in 1919 within the Hong Kong Volunteers, a virtual map of the Scottish stake in imperial commercial enterprise in Asia might be drawn.

Adam McGregor
A Personal Story

The story of Adam McGregor's short life links two of the themes of this book. When he was killed in action on 6 June 1915, Private McGregor was a Scotsman serving in a Scottish battalion of an English infantry regiment, and therefore part of the phenomenon of the migrant Scottish military tradition within the United Kingdom itself. But he is also representative of the homeward movement of Scottish emigrants living outside the British empire who came back to volunteer for service when war was declared. In 1914, Adam McGregor was resident in the United States of America, working in a wool-importing business in Denver, Colorado. Responding to his sense of duty towards the country of his birth and upbringing, and doubtless with something of the spirit of adventure which had taken him to Colorado in the first place, he sailed for Liverpool on board the Cunard liner RMS *Lusitania*, the ship which months later was to be torpedoed and sunk by a German submarine in the notorious incident which re-focused public attention in the USA on the war in Europe.

McGregor was a native of Kilmarnock, Ayrshire, where his father, also Adam, had a photography business in the town's King Street. Adam junior attended Kilmarnock Academy, where he was a member of the school's cadet corps, and went on to serve as a part-time Territorial Force volunteer soldier in the local regiment, the Royal Scots Fusiliers. The date of his emigration to the USA is unknown, but he went independently of his family. He might be characterised as a temporary migrant, or 'sojourner', moving across continents in search of independence, better prospects and life experience, and with the attractive asset of a Scottish education to offer employers. Had war not intervened, McGregor's longer-term future might have lain in America, but this, of course, must remain a matter for speculation.

What is striking about McGregor's return is that his previous service with the Royal Scots Fusiliers did not lead him to complete his journey home to Kilmarnock in order to enlist. Arriving in Liverpool on the

Below:

Private Adam McGregor of Denver, Colorado, in the uniform of the Liverpool Scottish.

© National Museums Scotland

142

Lusitania, he chose instead to join the local Scottish Territorial battalion, the 10th (Scottish) Battalion, King's (Liverpool) Regiment, otherwise known as the 'Liverpool Scottish'. This unit owed its existence to networks of prosperous and influential Scots in the commercial and professional life of the port city, who had first raised Scottish companies of local rifle volunteers in the 1860s from among the employees of merchants, brokers, ship-owning and sugar-refining firms with Scottish connections. After falling into abeyance for a time, the Scottish volunteering idea was revived in Liverpool during the South African War, and endured thereafter on a more permanent footing first as a Volunteer battalion and, from 1908, as a Territorial Force battalion of the King's (Liverpool) Regiment. The ranks of the Liverpool Scottish might have appealed to a young man of McGregor's enterprise and lower-middle-class background. Like certain other Territorial Force units of self-consciously exclusive character (the London Scottish among them), the Liverpool Scottish battalion had maintained in the immediate pre-war years entry requirements which included, as well as Scottish ancestry, the payment of an admission fee, and the stipulation that the entrant be from a non-manual 'white-collar' occupational background. While these stipulations were relaxed in 1914 in order to bring in fresh volunteers for war service, McGregor's education and occupation would have been received with approval.

It is possible of course that McGregor had reasons of his own for joining the Liverpool Scottish. He was far from being the only recruit

Below:

Men of the Liverpool Scottish in the rest area at 'Scottish Wood', St Eloi, Flanders, May 1915.

© National Museums Scotland

who made an international voyage in order to enlist in the battalion.[29] He might have wished to join up with friends, or might indeed have deduced that enlistment in Liverpool offered the fastest possible route into action, without the complication of a temporary return to Ayrshire. When he attested for service in Liverpool on 14 December 1914, the battalion was already on active service at Kemmel in Flanders, in trench lines as yet crudely developed in this first winter of the war.

By summer 1915 McGregor had joined his battalion in the Ypres salient, and was therefore in the line when the Liverpool Scottish conducted its first major attack, at the village of Hooge on 16 June 1915. In a frontal assault which won ground at terrible cost, Private Adam McGregor was one of 160 officers and men of the Liverpool Scottish killed outright on that day. He has no known grave and his name is one of nearly 55,000 of the missing inscribed on the Menin Gate memorial at Ypres (now Ieper). Amongst a small collection of photographs and correspondence at National Museums Scotland relating to Adam McGregor is a memorial card, printed on behalf of his parents in Kilmarnock on the first anniversary of his death for distribution among family and friends, acknowledging expressions of sympathy received. In Gothic script he is remembered as 'Adam McGregor, Aged 24 Years. Private, 10th King's Liverpool Scottish, and late of Denver, Colorado, U.S.A.'.[30]

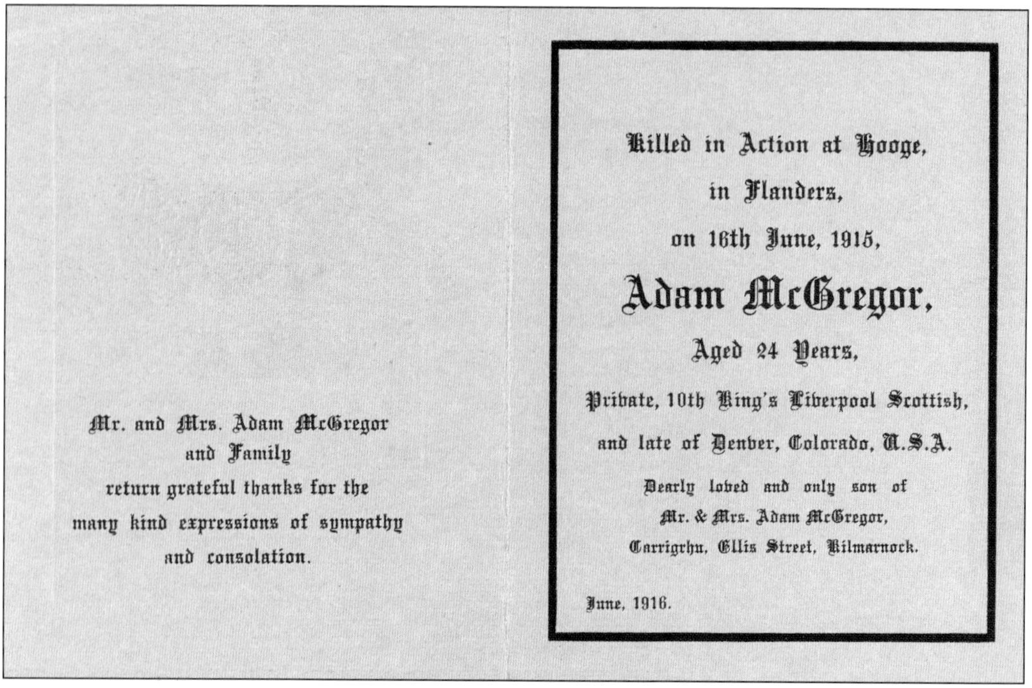

Mr. and Mrs. Adam McGregor
and Family
return grateful thanks for the
many kind expressions of sympathy
and consolation.

Killed in Action at Hooge,
in Flanders,
on 16th June, 1915,
Adam McGregor,
Aged 24 Years,
Private, 10th King's Liverpool Scottish,
and late of Denver, Colorado, U.S.A.
Dearly loved and only son of
Mr. & Mrs. Adam McGregor,
Carrigrhu, Ellis Street, Kilmarnock.
June, 1916.

Below:

Family memorial card for Adam McGregor, 1916.

© National Museums Scotland

Notes

1. Fraser Brown, 'Argentine Scots of the Great War', *The Red Hackle* 141, May 2014, pp. 23–4. The authors are grateful to Lieutenant-Colonel R. M. Riddell for drawing their attention to this article.
2. Nicholson [1964], p. 282.
3. Paul Gough, 'Sites in the imagination: the Beaumont Hamel Newfoundland Memorial on the Somme', *Cultural Geographies*, 11, 2004, 235–58.
4. Calder 2006, p. 5.
5. Devine 2011, p. 18.
6. Nicholson [1964], pp. 144–5. Original press report in the *Scotsman*, 2 September 1954.
7. *Ibid.*, 592.
8. David MacKenzie, 'Eastern Approaches: Maritime Canada and Newfoundland', in MacKenzie (ed.) 2005, p. 351.
9. W. David Parsons, 'Newfoundland and the Great War', in Busch (ed.) 2003, p. 147.
10. Parsons, 'Newfoundland and the Great War', in Busch (ed.) 2003, p. 148; and MacKenzie (ed.) 2005, p. 351.
11. Parsons, 'Newfoundland and the Great War', in Busch (ed.) 2003, p. 148.
12. Nicholson [1964], p. 110.
13. Quoted in Parsons, 'Newfoundland and the Great War', in Busch (ed.) 2003, p. 148.
14. *Ibid.*
15. Nicholson [1964], p. 128.
16. Figures quoted in Parsons, 'Newfoundland and the Great War' in Busch (ed.) 2003, pp. 150, 157.
17. *Ibid.*, 157–8.
18. National Museums Scotland: M.N1979.237.
19. Wilkinson 1999, p. 107.
20. Cox 2013, p. 146.
21. Elizabeth Buettner, 'Haggis in the Raj: private and public celebrations of Scottishness in late Imperial India', *Scottish Historical Review* 81, 2, 212, October 2002, pp. 212–39.
22. Major H. Browne, 'The early days of the Calcutta Scottish', *Calcutta Scottish Regimental Chronicle* 1, 1, Apr. 1933, pp. 3–5: and 'History of the Calcutta Scottish', *Calcutta Scottish Regimental Chronicle* 2,1, Aug. 1933, pp. 2–11; 3,1, Dec. 1933, pp. 1–7.
23. Press cuttings in E. A. Campbell [Collection of notes and illustrations of the Calcutta Scottish, 1914–37], unpub. notes, n.d. (*c.*1937) National Museums Scotland libraries, Library of the National War Museum, Edinburgh Castle, 3836.
24. Heathcote 1974, pp. 74–5. A cap badge of the Bengal and North Western Railway Rifle Volunteers, which consists of a Scottish saltire resting on a thistle leaf; National Museums Scotland acc. no. M.2001.66.
25. Biographical details from obituary notice in *British Medical Journal* 1, 3511, 21 April 1928, p. 696.
26. Heathcote, *The Military in British India: the Development of British Land Forces in South Asia, 1600–1947* (Manchester), pp. 202–3
27. National Museums Scotland: M.1953.350.1–2
28. Major H. Browne, 'History of the Calcutta Scottish', *Calcutta Scottish Regimental Chronicle* 2,1,1933, pp. 2–11.
29. Giblin 2000, pp. 7, 33.
30. National Museums Scotland, acc. no M.1993.699.8.

Bibliography

Calder, Jenni 2006. *The Scots in Canada* (Edinburgh).

Busch, Briton C. (ed.) 2003. *Canada and the Great War* (Montreal and Kingston).

Cox, Anthony 2013. *Empire, Industry and Class. The Imperial Nexus of Jute, 1840–1940* (Abingdon).

Devine, T. M. 2011. *To the Ends of the Earth* (London).

Giblin, Hal, with David Evans and Dennis Reeves 2000. *Bravest of Hearts. The Biography of a Battalion. The Liverpool Scottish in the Great War* (Liverpool).

Heathcote, T. A. 1974. *The Indian Army, The Garrison of Imperial India, 1822–1922* (London).

Heathcote, T. A. 1995. *The Military in British India: the Development of British Land Forces in South Asia, 1600–1947* (Manchester).

MacKenzie, David (ed.) 2005. *Canada and the First World War: Essays in Honour of Robert Craig Brown* (Toronto).

Nicholson, G. W. L. [1964]. *The Fighting Newfoundlander: A History of the Royal Newfoundland Regiment* (St John's, Newfoundland).

Wilkinson, Wynard R. T. 1999. *Indian Silver 1858–1947* (London).

Featured objects

Silver statuette of the Newfoundland Memorial at Beaumont Hamel on the Somme. On loan from the Royal Scots Regimental Museum. National Museums Scotland loan no. IL. 2014.7.

Plaid brooch of an officer of the Calcutta Scottish, 1914–20. National Museums Scotland acc. no. M.1932.756.

EPILOGUE

WHEN THE SCHEME FOR A SCOTTISH NATIONAL WAR
Memorial in Edinburgh Castle reached fruition in 1927, its philosophical
approach to commemoration was established not only in architecture
and iconography, but also through the ambitious task of compiling and
maintaining, in one place, the rolls of honour of the Scottish dead. The
scheme gathered to its shrine not only the names of the fallen from within the population of Scotland itself, but also the names of men from
every corner of the world who by dint of parentage, or through service in
a Scottish unit of whatever national origin, were identified as belonging
in its Books of Remembrance. Within the Memorial's focal point, the
Shrine, the imperial nature of the commemorative vision was reflected in
the heraldic carving of a 'Tree of Empire' with branches bearing the arms
of India and the Dominions, which an official commentator related to
'the Empire Overseas from which Scotsmen came to serve their Mother-
land'.[1] The Shrine's bronze frieze, a procession of figures representing the
totality of Scottish participation in the war effort, incorporated figures
from the Dominion and Anglo-Scottish regiments.[2]

In the Hall of Honour, between the bays dedicated to the old Scottish regiments, were placed smaller inscribed dedications situated below
sculpted trophies of arms:

*To Scotsmen of all ranks who fell serving with units of the British
Dominions and Colonies 1914–1918,*

*To the memory of officers & other ranks of Scottish descent who fell
serving in the Indian Army during the Great War 1914–1918,*

*To Scotsmen of all ranks who fell serving with English, Irish and
Welsh regiments 1914–1918.*

On piers close to these catch-all dedications were added small unit
memorials in bronze, with Books of Remembrance in each instance, for
the 16th (Canadian Scottish) Battalion, for the South African Scottish
Battalion, and for the battalions of the London, Liverpool and Tyneside
Scottish. Above them a carving of a soldier standing by a grave carried
the Gaelic inscription: '*Mo Dhuthaich: M'onoir: is Mo Dhia* [*My Country, My Honour, My God*]. Further Books of Remembrance completed
the commemoration of the Scottish dead from the expeditionary forces
of Canada, Australia and New Zealand.

Old Scotland's claim upon the New World fallen was uncontrover-
sial. If it entailed double-counting alongside the rolls of honour of the
respective Dominions, this was tacitly taken as a natural and positive
expression of the ties of family and empire. For the establishment figures
behind the raising of the Memorial, Scottish sacrifice in the Great War
rested within the continuum of Scottish history and was also an affirma-

Opening page:

Emigrants bound for
Canada in the Clyde-built
SS *Minnedosa* 1925.

© Hulton-Deutsch
Collection/Corbis

147

tion of the unity of the British empire. One like-minded and influential individual was John Buchan, the foremost popular contemporary historian of the war.[3] Among his many official and unofficial propagandist writing ventures was a sequence of historical accounts published during the war in the *Glasgow Herald* newspaper, which were collected together into a booklet *The Battle Honours of Scotland* published in 1919. Regretting that the limitations of the format allowed only a sketch based on stories of 'the actual Scottish units', Buchan acknowledged that this was not the full story, averring that ...

> *The Canadian Corps was largely Scottish, there was a big Scottish element in the Australian and New Zealand divisions, the heroic South African Brigade on the Western Front had one wholly Scottish battalion and many Scots in the others.*[4]

With his Scottish background, his earlier career in South Africa, and his fervent attachment to an ideal of the moral integrity and vigour of the British imperial races, Buchan may be forgiven a tendency to Scottish hyperbole in this context and in the admission, which followed, in a passage on the battle at Delville Wood, that 'I may be prejudiced but after a Scot I prefer a South African, who indeed, in nine cases out of ten is of Scottish blood'.[5] In formulating the *Common Cause* exhibition, and writing this book to accompany it, the present authors were aware that they ran the risk of reinforcing ideas about Scottish exceptionalism in military endeavour without due sense of proportion. However significant migration may have been in the social, economic and cultural history of Scotland, it is worth repeating here that Scotland is estimated to have accounted for only 8% of total nineteenth-century migration from Great Britain and Ireland. It needs to be borne in mind that the overwhelming majority of the volunteer auxiliary forces of the Dominions and colonies of the British empire, and all the units of their wartime expeditionary forces, did *not* adopt Scottish traditional identities. It could indeed be argued that this majority was instead expressing Englishness and English military traditions in relation to British imperial identity and their own developing sense of nationhood. Furthermore, the Scottish overseas battalions from Canada and South Africa had Irish equivalents, albeit at a more modest scale and without the flamboyant material culture to mark them out.[6]

If this argument is extended with reference to material and visual culture, it is a corrective to observe, for example, just how British in their imagery were many of the posters released by the Canadian government to encourage voluntary recruitment, subscription to war funds, and other patriotic endeavours. The Scottish military iconography of recruiting posters released by Scottish battalions of the Canadian Expeditionary Force needs to be seen in this overall context, being only a modest proportion of a total which included Union flags, French cultural references for appeal to the French Canadian population, Irish appeals and images of idealised frontier life specific to Canada. Nevertheless, one official Great War poster catches the eye, an example of which is now in the collections of the Canadian War Museum.[7] Printed in 1918 in London, the imperial capital, this poster is entitled *The British Commonwealth in Arms* and represents the war effort of the British Dominions, alongside that of Great Britain, by using the figure of an individual soldier to stand for each. Britain is represented by a 'Tommy', a British infantryman in service dress uniform, as is Newfoundland. The equivalent figures representing Australia and New Zealand are distinguished by their 'slouch hat' and 'lemon squeezer' national headgear respectively. But for both Canada and South Africa, national identity is expressed in the choice of figures of infantrymen wearing kilt and Scottish bonnet. This choice might have appealed from a graphic design point of view, making for a more varied imagery, but it also suggests that impartial contemporary observers were prepared to accept the correlation between Scottish military traditions, Canada and South Africa as a norm.

Above:

Propaganda poster, with Canada and South Africa represented by Scottish soldiers, 1918.

CWM 19900348-004
© Canadian War Museum

The purpose of this book has been to explore the relationships between Scottish migration, the British Commonwealth and the Great War through the medium of material culture. It must be noted in conclusion that the relationship was self-reinforcing since after the interregnum of the war years, during which young men of Scottish birth or descent had flowed back towards Europe to fight, levels of emigration from Scotland started to increase once again, to such an extent that throughout the 1920s two-thirds of all British emigrants were Scots. The effects of the war included both social dislocation and a huge increase in the fluidity of the Scottish population. Despite a natural increase of 7.2%, the increase in migration from Scotland left the population balance sheet 0.8% in the red. Scotland faced a demographic crisis.[8]

There was also a crisis of confidence. Disillusionment with the Scotland of the 1920s was widely felt, not least by many of those who had fought in the Great War. One of those not content with his lot was Ronald Dewar, a former lance corporal in 7th Battalion Cameron Highlanders. A man of Scottish nationalist sympathies, Dewar grew frustrated with the lack of prospects at home and chose to leave for the United States of America. Before departing, he typed up a collection of verse of his own composition for presentation to his friend and wartime platoon comrade Douglas Wilson.[9] Among lines recalling shared battle experiences at Martinpuich and Arras, Wilson also penned 'Verses for the Scots National League', an address from a war veteran to one of the forerunners of the National Party of Scotland, commencing with the lines:

> *Still do the hills of Scotland fling*
> *Their heads above the sheltered straths,*
> *And still the Scottish rivers sing*
> *Along their old appointed paths.*
> *All outwardly is much the same*
> *As known by our remembered dead,*
> *We have the country and the name,*
> *But where has Scotland's spirit fled?*

The outflow from Scotland benefited the Dominion nations as well as the United States, as they too emerged from the war seeking to tackle the challenges of the new decade. In this they had the support of the British government, which passed the Empire Settlement Act of 1922 providing assisted passage to encourage migration to the Dominions rather than to the USA.[10] The latter remained a destination of choice nonetheless, on a par with Canada and well ahead of Australia and New Zealand, with South Africa some way behind. The imagery of social and economic dislocation in post-war Scotland revolves around political discord in the industrial west, 'Red Clydeside' and tanks on the streets in the 'battle of George Square'.[11] However, these dramatic events masked the demographic realities where loss of population was most keenly felt in the Highland counties, a situation which sharply contrasted with the late-nineteenth and early-twentieth century exodus from the industrial belt of lowland Scotland.[12]

In the inter-war years there was a marked recrudescence in Scottish emigrant military tradition in the reserve forces of the Dominions, in the establishment of new Scottish units, the re-badging of existing units as Scottish, and in the proliferation of inter-diasporic affiliations. In Canada a whole new phalanx of kilted regiments appeared, often through name changes and amalgamations, as the Canadian militia went through a period of reorganisation.[13] The drive to establish Scottish military units continued well into the 1930s and right across the global reach of the diaspora, where 'the potency of the Highland soldier image ... endured'.[14] In Australia, for example, an appeal was made in 1935 to 'Australian Citizens of Scottish Birth and Lineage' for 'the encouragement, support and maintenance of an Australian Scottish Kilted Regiment'.[15] Military associationalism was a robust re-affirmation of the 'age-old bond between the identity of the Scottish nation, empire and the military tradition'.[16] The political changes and critiques emerging in post-war Scotland were not mirrored in its diasporic world; the various Caledonian or St Andrew's societies did not prove fertile recruiting grounds for the incipient Scottish nationalist movement.[17] As one Scots Australian politician, J. MacCallum Smith MLA of Western Australia, was reported to have said, presumably with no sense of contradiction, 'the Scottish societies in Australia had no politics – their only policy was the maintenance of the British Empire'.[18]

Fuelled by the increased number of emigrants from the home country, Scottish associational activity thrived in the period after the Great War. In Australia there was a proliferation of new Caledonian societies from 1919 to 1935, particularly in the rapidly expanding suburban enclaves of urban areas.[19] However, in Canada the further rise of associationalism would be offset after many Scots opted to return home in the years after the Wall Street Crash of 1929.[20] The global economic crisis of the inter-war period meant that for many Scottish migrants their dreams of a better future were not realised. And as economic depression slipped into political crisis in Europe, it was not long before the Scottish military units of the British empire were once again channelling recruits towards a world war.

Below:

Unit memorials in the Scottish National War Memorial.

Antonia Reeve and Trustees of the Scottish National War Memorial

Notes

1 Weaver 1927, p. 11.
2 Deas 1927, pp. 20–4.
3 John Buchan delivered his 24-volume *Nelson's History of the War*, between 1915 and 1919. For an account of Buchan's wartime activities as novelist, official propagandist and historian, see Hew Strachan 'John Buchan and the First World War: fact into fiction', *War in History*, 2009, 16 (3), pp. 298–324.
4 Buchan 1919, p. 6.
5 *Ibid.*, p. 20.
6 For example, a 121st (Western Irish) Battalion, a 158th (Duke of Connaught's Own) Battalion, a 199th (Duchess of Connaught's Own Irish Rangers) Battalion and a 208th (Canadian Irish) Battalion, were recruited for the Canadian Expeditionary Force; while the South African Irish served as a Citizen Force unit with Union forces in German South-West Africa in 1914–15.
7 Canadian War Museum Propaganda Poster, CWM 19900348-004.
8 Harper 1998, p. 6.
9 National Museums Scotland acc. no. M.2014.5.
10 Cameron 2010, p. 126.
11 Marwick 2006, pp. 313–4.
12 Harper 1998, p. 4.
13 George F. G. Stanley, 'The Scottish Military Tradition', in Stanford Reid 1976, p. 151.
14 Wendy Ugolini, 'Scottish Commonwealth Regiments', in Spiers, Crang and Strickland (eds), p. 496.
15 Buckley 1986, p. 68.
16 T. M. Devine, 'Soldiers of Empire', in MacKenzie and Devine 2011, p. 195.
17 Harper 1998, p. 204.
18 Quoted in Prentis, *The Scots in Australia*, p. 203.
19 Prentis 2008, pp. 201–2.
20 Baines 1995, p. 69.

Bibliography

Baines, Dudley 1995. *Emigration from Europe* (Cambridge).

Buchan, John 1919. *The Battle Honours of Scotland, 1914–18* (Glasgow).

Buckley, Martin J. 1986. *Scarlet and Tartan: the story of the regiments and regimental bands of the NSW Scottish Rifles (Volunteers), the 30th Battalion (NSW Scottish Regiment), 'A' Company and Pipes and Drums, 17th Battalion, Royal New South Wales Regiment* (Sydney).

Cameron, Ewen A. 2010. *Impaled Upon a Thistle: Scotland since 1880* (Edinburgh).

Deas, F. W. 1927. *The Scottish National War Memorial Official Guide* (Edinburgh).

Harper, Marjory 1998. *Emigration from Scotland between the Wars* (Manchester).

MacKenzie, John M. and T. M. Devine (eds) 2011. *Scotland and the British Empire* (Oxford).

Marwick, Arthur 2006. *The Deluge: British Society and the First World War*, 2nd edition (London).

Prentis, Malcolm 2008, *The Scots in Australia* (Sydney).

Spiers, Edward M., Jeremy A Crang and Matthew J. Strickland (eds) 2012. *A Military History of Scotland* (Edinburgh).

Stanford Reid, W. 1976. *The Scottish Tradition in Canada* (Toronto).

Weaver, Sir Lawrence 1927. *The Scottish National War Memorial. The Castle, Edinburgh. A Record and Appreciation* (London).